The New City Catechism
Devotional

The New City Catechism

Devotional

God's Truth for Our
Hearts and Minds

Introduction by
Timothy Keller

Collin Hansen,
General Editor

CROSSWAY®

WHEATON, ILLINOIS

Trade paperback ISBN: 978-1-4335-5503-9
ePub ISBN: 978-1-4335-5506-0
PDF ISBN: 978-1-4335-5504-6
Mobipocket ISBN: 978-1-4335-5505-3

Library of Congress Cataloging-in-Publication Data

Names: Hansen, Collin, 1981– editor.
Title: The new city catechism devotional : God's truth for our hearts and minds / introduction by Timothy Keller ; Collin Hansen, general editor.
Description: Wheaton : Crossway, 2017. | Includes bibliographical references.
Identifiers: LCCN 2016038579 (print) | LCCN 2017005993 (ebook) | ISBN 9781433555039 (hc) | ISBN 9781433555046 (pdf) | ISBN 9781433555053 (mobi) | ISBN 9781433555060 (epub)
Subjects: LCSH: New city catechism. | Presbyterian Church—Catechisms—English. | Reformed Church—Catechisms—English. | Christian education of children. | Westminster Assembly (1643–1652). Shorter catechism.
Classification: LCC BX9184.N493 N49 2017 (print) | LCC BX9184.N493 (ebook) | DDC 238/.51—dc23
LC record available at https://lccn.loc.gov/2016038579

VP   27   26   25   24   23   22   21   20   19   18   17
15   14   13   12   11   10   9   8   7   6   5   4

Contents

Introduction

TIMOTHY KELLER

Question 1. What is the chief end of man?
Answer. Man's chief end is to glorify God and to enjoy him forever.

Question 1. What is your only comfort in life and death?
Answer. That I am not my own, but belong—body and soul, in life and in death—to my faithful Savior, Jesus Christ.

These words, the opening of the Westminster and Heidelberg catechisms, find echoes in many of our creeds and statements of faith. They are familiar to us from sermons and books, and yet most people do not know their source and have certainly never memorized them as part of the catechisms from which they derive.

Today many churches and Christian organizations publish "statements of faith" that outline their beliefs. But in the past it was expected that documents of this nature would be so biblically rich and carefully crafted that they would be memorized and used for Christian growth and training. They were written in the form of questions and answers, and were called *catechisms* (from the Greek *katechein*, which means "to teach orally or to instruct by word of mouth"). The Heidelberg Catechism of 1563 and Westminster Shorter and Larger catechisms of 1648 are among the best known, and they serve as the doctrinal standards of many churches in the world today.

The Lost Practice of Catechesis

At present, the practice of catechesis, particularly among adults, has been almost completely lost. Modern discipleship programs concentrate on practices such as Bible study, prayer, fellowship, and evangelism and can at times be superficial when it comes to doctrine. In contrast, the classic catechisms take students through the Apostles' Creed, the Ten Commandments, and the Lord's Prayer—a perfect balance of biblical theology, practical ethics, and spiritual experience. Also, the catechetical discipline of memorization drives concepts deeper into the heart and naturally holds students more accountable to master the material than do typical discipleship courses. Finally, the practice of question-answer recitation brings instructors and students into a naturally interactive, dialogical process of learning.

In short, catechetical instruction is less individualistic and more communal. Parents can catechize their children. Church leaders can catechize new members with shorter catechisms and new leaders with more extensive ones. Because of the richness of the material, catechetical questions and answers may be integrated into corporate worship itself, where the church as a body can confess their faith and respond to God with praise.

Because we have lost the practice of catechesis today, "superficial smatterings of truth, blurry notions about God and godliness, and thoughtlessness about the issues of living—career-wise, community-wise, family-wise, and church-wise—are all too often the marks of evangelical congregations today."[1]

Why Write New Catechisms?

There are many ancient, excellent, and time-tested catechisms. Why expend the effort to write new ones? In fact, some people might suspect the motives of anyone who would want to do so. However, most people today do not realize that it was once seen as normal, important, and necessary for churches to continually produce new catechisms for their own use. The original Anglican *Book of Common Prayer* included a catechism. The Lutheran churches had Luther's Large Catechism and Small Catechism of 1529. The early Scottish churches, though they had Calvin's Geneva Catechism of 1541 and the Heidelberg Catechism of 1563, went on to produce and use Craig's Catechism of 1581, Duncan's Latin Catechism of 1595, and the New Catechism of 1644, before eventually adopting the Westminster Catechism.

Puritan pastor Richard Baxter, who ministered in the seventeenth-century town of Kidderminster, wanted to systematically train heads of families to instruct their households in the faith. To do so he wrote his own Family Catechism that was adapted to the capacities of his people and that brought the Bible to bear on many of the issues and questions his people were facing at that time.

Catechisms were written with at least three purposes. The first was to set forth a comprehensive exposition of the gospel—not only in order to explain clearly what the gospel is, but also to lay out the building blocks on which the gospel is based, such as the biblical doctrines of God, of human nature, of sin, and so forth. The second purpose was to do this exposition in such a way that the heresies, errors, and false beliefs of the time and culture were addressed and counteracted. The third and more pastoral purpose was to form a distinct people, a counterculture that reflected the likeness of Christ not only in individual character but also in the church's communal life.

When looked at together, these three purposes explain why new catechisms must be written. While our exposition of gospel doctrine must be in line with older catechisms that are true to the Word, culture changes, and so do the errors, temptations, and challenges to the unchanging gospel that people must be equipped to face and answer.

Structure of *The New City Catechism*

The New City Catechism comprises only 52 questions and answers (as opposed to Heidelberg's 129 or Westminster Shorter's 107). There is therefore only one question and answer for each week of the year, making it simple to fit into church calendars and achievable for people with demanding schedules.

The New City Catechism is based on and adapted from Calvin's Geneva Catechism, the Westminster Shorter and Larger catechisms, and especially the Heidelberg Catechism. This gives good exposure to some of the riches and insights across the spectrum of the great Reformation-era catechisms, the hope being that it will encourage people to delve into the historic catechisms and continue the catechetical process throughout their lives.

It is divided into three parts to make it easier to learn in sections and to include some helpful divisions:

Part 1: God, creation and fall, law (twenty questions)
Part 2: Christ, redemption, grace (fifteen questions)
Part 3: Spirit, restoration, growing in grace (seventeen questions)

As with most traditional catechisms, a Bible verse accompanies each question and answer. In addition, each question and answer is followed by a short commentary taken from the writings or sayings of a past preacher as well as a commentary from a contemporary preacher to help students meditate on and think about the topic being explored. Each question ends with a short, original prayer.

The Use of Archaic Language

Although it may make the content seem less accessible at first glance, the language of the original texts has been retained as much as possible throughout the historical commentaries. When people complained to J. R. R. Tolkien about the archaic language he sometimes used, he answered that language carries cultural values, and therefore his use of older forms was not nostalgia—it was principled. He believed that older ways of speaking conveyed older ways of understanding life that modern forms cannot convey, because modern language is enmeshed with modern views of life.

For this reason, except in cases where the words are no longer in common use and are therefore incomprehensible (in which instances they often have been replaced with ellipses), the language and spelling of the original authors have been retained throughout the historic commentaries. Occasionally this language is also reflected in the questions and answers where the more poetic forms aid memorization.

How to Use *The New City Catechism*

The New City Catechism consists of fifty-two questions and answers, so the easiest way to use it is to memorize one question and answer each week of the year. Because it is intended to be dialogical, it is best to learn it in pairs, in families, or as study groups, enabling you to drill one another on the answers not only one at a time but once you have learned ten of them, then twenty of them, and so on.

The Bible verse, written commentary, and prayer that are attached to each question and answer can be used as your devotion on a chosen day of the week to help you think through and meditate on the issues and applications that arise from the question and answer.

Groups may decide to spend the first five to ten minutes of their study time looking together at only one question and answer, thus completing the catechism in a year, or they may prefer to study and learn the questions and answers over a contracted length of time, for example by memorizing five or six questions a week and meeting together to quiz one another and discuss them, as well as read the accompanying commentaries.

Memorization Tips

There are a variety of ways to commit texts to memory, and some techniques suit certain learning styles better than others. A few examples include:

- Read the question and answer out loud, and repeat, repeat, repeat.
- Read the question and answer out loud, then try to repeat them without looking. Repeat.
- Read aloud all part 1 questions and answers (then part 2, then part 3) while physically moving about. The combination of movement and speech strengthens a person's ability to recall text.
- Record yourself saying all part 1 questions and answers (then part 2, then part 3) and listen to them during everyday activities such as workouts, chores, and so on.

- Write the questions and answers on cards and tape them in a conspicuous area. Read them aloud every time you see them.
- Make flash cards with the question on one side and the answer on the other, and test yourself.
- Write out the question and answer. Repeat. The process of writing helps a person's ability to recall text.
- Drill the questions and answers with another person as often as possible.

A Biblical Practice

In his letter to the Galatians Paul writes, "Let the one who is taught the word share all good things with the one who teaches" (Gal. 6:6). The Greek word for "the one who is taught" is *katechoumenos*, one who is catechized. In other words, Paul is talking about a body of Christian doctrine (*catechism*) that was taught to them by an instructor (here the word *catechizer*). The words "all good things" probably mean financial support as well. In this light, the word *koinoneo*—which means "to share" or "to have fellowship"—becomes even richer. The salary of a Christian teacher is not to be seen simply as a payment but a "fellowship." Catechesis is not just one more service to be paid for, but is a rich fellowship and mutual sharing of the gifts of God.

If we re-engage in this biblical practice in our churches, we will find again God's Word "dwelling in us richly" (see Col. 3:16), because the practice of catechesis takes truth deep into our hearts, so we think in biblical categories as soon as we can reason.

When my son Jonathan was a young child, my wife, Kathy, and I started teaching him a children's catechism. In the beginning we worked on just the first three questions:

Question 1. Who made you?
Answer. God

Question 2. What else did God make?
Answer. God made all things.

Question 3. Why did God make you and all things?
Answer. For his own glory.

One day Kathy dropped Jonathan off at a babysitter's. At one point the babysitter discovered Jonathan looking out the window. "What are you thinking about?" she asked him. "God," he said. Surprised, she responded, "What are you thinking about God?" He looked at her and replied, "How he made all things for his own glory." She thought she had a spiritual giant on her hands! A little boy looking out the window, contemplating the glory of God in creation!

What had actually happened, obviously, was that her question had triggered the question/answer response in him. He answered with the catechism. He certainly did not have the slightest idea what the "glory of God" meant. But the concept was in his mind and heart, waiting to be connected with new insights, teaching, and experiences.

Such instruction, Princeton theologian Archibald Alexander said, is like firewood in a fireplace. Without the fire—the Spirit of God—firewood will not in itself produce a warming flame. But without fuel there can be no fire either, and that is what catechetical instruction is.

Part 1

God, Creation and Fall, Law

Question 1

What is our only hope in life and death?

That we are not our own but belong, body and soul, both in life and death, to God and to our Savior Jesus Christ.

📖 ROMANS 14:7–8

For none of us lives to himself, and none of us dies to himself. For if we live, we live to the Lord, and if we die, we die to the Lord. So then, whether we live or whether we die, we are the Lord's.

💬 Commentary

JOHN CALVIN

If we, then, are not our own but the Lord's, it is clear what error we must flee, and whither we must direct all the acts of our life. We are not our own: let not our reason nor our will, therefore, sway our plans and deeds. We are not our own: let us therefore not set it as our goal to seek what is expedient for us. . . . We are not our own: in so far as we can, let us forget ourselves and all that is ours. Conversely, we are God's: let us therefore live for him and die for him. We are

God's: let his wisdom and will therefore rule all our actions. We are God's: let all the parts of our life accordingly strive toward him as our only lawful goal. O, how much has that man profited who, having been taught that he is not his own, has taken away dominion and rule from his own reason that he may yield it to God! For, as consulting our self-interest is the pestilence that most effectively leads to our destruction, so the sole haven of salvation is to be wise in nothing and to will nothing through ourselves but to follow the leading of the Lord alone.[2]

TIMOTHY KELLER

At one point in his writings John Calvin lays out the essence of what it means to live the Christian life. He says that he could make us a list of the commandments we should be keeping or a list of all the character traits we should be exhibiting. But instead, he wants to boil it down to the basic motive and the basic principle of what it means to live the Christian life.

The basic motive is that God sent his Son to save us by grace and to adopt us into his family. So now, because of that grace, in our gratitude, we want to resemble our Father. We want the family resemblance. We want to look like our Savior. We want to please our Father.

The basic principle then is this: that we are not to live to please ourselves. We're not to live as if we belong to ourselves. And that means several things. It means, first of all, we are not to determine for ourselves what is right or wrong. We give up the right to determine that, and we rely wholly on God's Word. We also give up the operating principle that we usually use in day-to-day life; we stop putting ourselves first, and we always put first what pleases God and what loves our neighbor. It also means that we are to have no part of our lives that is immune from self-giving. We're supposed to give ourselves wholly to him—body and soul. And it means we trust God through thick and thin, through the good and the bad times, in life and in death.

And how do the motive and the principle relate? Because we're saved by grace, we're not our own. A woman once said to me, "If I knew I was saved because of what I did, if I contributed to my salvation, then God couldn't ask anything of me because I'd made a contribution. But if I'm saved by grace, sheer grace, then there's nothing he cannot ask of me." And that's right. You're not your own. You were bought with a price.

Some years ago I heard a Christian speaker say, "How can you come to grips with someone who has given himself utterly for you without you giving yourself utterly for him?"

Jesus gave himself wholly for us. So now, we must give ourselves wholly to him.

🤲 Prayer

Christ Our Hope, in life and in death, we cast ourselves on your merciful, fatherly care. You love us because we are your own. We have no good apart from you, and we could ask for no greater gift than to belong to you. Amen.

Question 2

What is God?

God is the creator and sustainer of everyone and everything. He is eternal, infinite, and unchangeable in his power and perfection, goodness and glory, wisdom, justice, and truth. Nothing happens except through him and by his will.

📖 PSALM 86:8–10, 15

There is none like you among the gods, O Lord,
   nor are there any works like yours.
All the nations you have made shall come
   and worship before you, O Lord,
and shall glorify your name.
   For you are great and do wondrous things;
   you alone are God. . . .
But you, O Lord, are a God merciful and gracious,
   slow to anger and abounding in steadfast love and
     faithfulness.

⊟ Commentary

JONATHAN EDWARDS

The Creator of the world is doubtless also the Governor of it. He that had power to give being to the world, and set all the parts of it in order, has doubtless power to dispose of the world, to continue the order he has constituted, or to alter it. He that first gave the laws of nature, must have all nature in his hands; so that it is evident God has the world in his hands, to dispose of as he pleases. . . .

And it is manifest, in fact, that God is not careless how the affairs and concerns of the world he has made proceed, because he was not careless of this matter in the creation itself; as it is apparent, by the manner and order in which things were created, that God, in creating, took care of the future progress and state of things in the world.[3]

D. A. CARSON

It is spectacularly wonderful to talk about God, to think about him. There cannot be any higher subject. But the word *God* itself is not an empty cipher. Just because somebody uses the word *God* and then somebody else uses the word *God*, it does not follow that they mean the same thing. God, for some, is an inexpressible feeling, or it's the unmoved cause at the beginning of the universe, or it's a being full of transcendence. But we're talking about the God of the Bible, and the God of the Bible is self-defined. He talks about himself as being eternal and righteous. He's the God of love. He's the God of transcendence; that is, he's above space and time and history. Yet he is the *immanent* God; that is, he is so much with us that we cannot possibly escape from him. He is everywhere. He is unchangeable. He is truthful. He is reliable. He's personal.

What's really important to see and understand, as God has disclosed himself not only in words but in the whole storyline of the Bible's narrative, is that we are not permitted to take one attribute of God and make everything of it. We cannot, let's say, take his sovereignty and forget his goodness. Or take his goodness and forget his holiness (his holiness is what makes him the God of judgment).

Or take his judgment, even the severity of his judgment, and forget that he's the God of love, the God who has so much loved even his rebellious creatures that ultimately he sent his Son to bear their sin in his own body on the tree.

In other words, to get to the heart of who God is and to bow before him in some small measure of genuine understanding, it's important to think through what the Bible says again and again and integrate the whole with the same balance and proportion that Scripture itself gives. That calls us to worship. And if we put anything else in the place of God, that is the very definition of idolatry.

🙏 Prayer

Our Creator and Sustainer, everything holds together in you. The smallest creature is known to you, and the mightiest army is at your command. You rule with justice. Help us to trust your goodness in all that you will. Amen.

Question 3

How many persons are there in God?

There are three persons in the one true and living God: the Father, the Son, and the Holy Spirit. They are the same in substance, equal in power and glory.

📖 2 CORINTHIANS 13:14

The grace of the Lord Jesus Christ and the love of God and the fellowship of the Holy Spirit be with you all.

💬 Commentary

RICHARD BAXTER

The great mystery of the Blessed Trinity, Father, Son, and Holy Ghost, being one God, is made necessary to us to be believed, not only as to the eternal unsearchable Inexistence, but especially for the knowledge of God's three great sorts of works on man: that is, as our Creator, and the God of nature; as our Redeemer, and the God of governing and reconciling grace; and as our Sanctifier, and the Applier and Perfecter of all to fit us to glory. . . .

God is one infinite, undivided Spirit; and yet that he is Father, Son, and Holy Ghost, must be believed. . . .

How is it to be proved that the Holy Ghost is God? We are to be baptized into the belief of him as of the Father and the Son, and in that he doth the works proper to God, and hath the attributes of God in Scripture.[4]

KEVIN DEYOUNG

The doctrine of the Trinity is the most important Christian doctrine that most people never think about. It's absolutely essential to our faith, and yet for many Christians it just seems like a very confusing math problem. And even if we can figure out what *Trinity* means, it doesn't feel like it has much bearing on our lives, much relevance to us.

The word *Trinity*, famously, is not found in the Bible, but the word does very well at capturing a number of biblical truths. There are actually seven statements that go into the doctrine of the Trinity:

1. God is one. There's only one God.
2. The Father is God.
3. The Son is God.
4. The Holy Spirit is God.
5. The Father is not the Son.
6. The Son is not the Spirit.
7. The Spirit is not the Father.

If you get those seven statements, then you've captured the doctrine of the Trinity—what it means when we say there is one God and three persons.

Christians are monotheists. We don't believe in many gods or a pantheon of gods but just one God, and this God expresses himself and exists as three persons. That language of *persons* is very important. The early church wrestled with the appropriate language, and *persons* aptly speaks to the personality of the three members of the Trinity and also their relationship with each other; the Father, Son, and Holy Spirit coinhere as one essence, and yet there are distinctions. One is not the other, but they're equal in rank, equal in power, equal in glory, equal in majesty. Just as Jesus sends out the disciples to go baptize in the name of the Father, and of the Son, and of the Holy Spirit, we see this doctrine of the Holy Trinity woven throughout the Scriptures.

Even more confusing to people is the question "Why does this even matter? Okay, I understand I got three in one, one in three. What difference does this make for anything in my Christian life?" In good Trinitarian fashion, I think there are three important things that the doctrine means for us.

First, the Trinity helps us to understand how there can be unity in diversity. This is one of the most pressing questions in our world. Some folks focus almost exclusively on diversity, on the fact that people are so different. They don't see any common ground. Others want to press for complete uniformity in thought, in government, and in expression. The Trinity shows us that you can have a profound, real, organic unity with diversity, so that the Father, Son, and Holy Spirit are working in complete union in our salvation. The Father appoints. The Son accomplished. The Spirit applies. We encounter God as fully God in the Father, in the Son, and in the Holy Spirit. And yet, their divine work is neither interchangeable nor redundant.

Second, when you have a triune God, you have the eternality of love. Love has existed from all time. If you have a god who is not three persons, he has to create a being to love, to be an expression of his love. But Father, Son, and Holy Spirit existing in eternity have always had this relationship of love. So love is not a created thing. God didn't have to go outside of himself to love. Love is eternal. And when you have a triune God, you have fully this God who is love.

Finally, and most importantly, the doctrine of the Trinity is crucial for the Christian because there is nothing more important in all the world than knowing God. If God exists as one God in three persons, if the one divine essence subsists as Father, Son, and Holy Spirit, if we are baptized into this triune name, then no Christian should want to be ignorant of these Trinitarian realities. In the end, the Trinity matters because God matters.

Prayer

Father, Son, and Spirit, you are beyond our understanding. Thank you for bringing us into your love, a love that existed before the world in your three perfect persons. Amen.

Question 4

How and why did
God create us?

God created us male and female in his own image to know him, love him, live with him, and glorify him. And it is right that we who were created by God should live to his glory.

📖 GENESIS 1:27

> So God created man in his own image,
>   in the image of God he created him;
>   male and female he created them.

💬 Commentary

J. C. RYLE

The glory of God is the first thing that God's children should desire. It is the object of one of our Lord's own prayers: "Father, glorify thy name" (John 12:28). It is the purpose for which the world was created. It is the end for which the saints are called and converted. It is the chief thing we should seek, that "God in all things may be glorified" (1 Pet. 4:11). . . .

Anything whereby we may glorify God is a talent, our gifts, our influence, our money, our knowledge, our health, our strength, our time, our senses, our reason, our intellect, our memory, our affections, our privileges as members of Christ's Church, our advantages as possessors of the Bible—all, all are talents. Whence came these things? What hand bestowed them? Why are we what we are? Why are we not the worms that crawl on the earth? There is only one answer to these questions. All that we have is a loan from God. We are God's stewards. We are God's debtors. Let this thought sink deeply into our hearts.[5]

JOHN PIPER

Why do people make images? People make images to *image*. They want to image forth something. If you make a statue of Napoleon, you want people to think not so much about the statue as Napoleon. And you make the statue in a way that shows something specific about the character of Napoleon.

So God makes us in his image. We could argue about whether it is our rationality, or our morality, or our volition that makes us in his image. The point is, he makes humans in his image to image something, namely, himself. So our existence is about showing God's existence or, specifically, it's about showing God's glory. Which I think means God's manifold perfections—the radiance, the display, the streaming out of his many-colored, beautiful perfections. We want to think and live and act and speak in such a way that we draw attention to the manifold perfections of God. And I think the way we do that best is by being totally satisfied in those perfections ourselves. They mean more to us than money and more to us than fame and more to us than sex or anything else that might compete for our affections. And when people see us valuing God that much and his glory being that satisfying, they see that he is our treasure. Show me more! I think that's what it means to glorify God by being in his image.

And the place where the glory is shown most clearly is the gospel where Christ dies; the Son of God dies for sinners. I say that because in 2 Corinthians 4:4 it says, "The god of this world," that's Satan, "has blinded the minds of unbelievers, to keep them from seeing the light of the gospel of the glory of Christ, who is the image of God." Do you want to know where the glory of God is shining most brightly? It is shining in Christ in the gospel most brightly. So if we want to be conformed fully into his image and display to others his glory, there's a verse just before that that says "beholding the glory of the Lord, [we] are being transformed into the same image from one degree of glory to another" (2 Cor. 3:18). And that comes from the Spirit.

So we look at Jesus, we treasure him, we love him, and in that we are being shaped into his image.

When God says he made us male and female to do this, not only does that mean we want generations to go on doing this, so there's going to be procreation here, but it means this happens best in community. It's not good for the man to be alone. Who's he going to glorify God to? So this little community that's created in the beginning called male and female is representative of the community where the glory of God radiates back and forth to each other and then out to the world.

Let's do this together. Let's help each other glorify God.

Prayer

Maker of All, let us not lose sight that we, and every human being you have made, are created in your image. Never let us doubt this about ourselves. Never let us doubt this about any other man or woman, for to do so denies you the glory that is due to your name. Your likeness glimpsed in us testifies that we belong to you, body and soul. Amen.

Question 5

What else did God create?

God created all things by his powerful Word, and all his creation was very good; everything flourished under his loving rule.

📖 **GENESIS 1:31**

And God saw everything that he had made, and behold, it was very good. . . .

💬 **Commentary**

JOHN CALVIN

God has given us, throughout the whole frame-work of this world, clear evidences of his eternal wisdom, goodness, and power; and though he is in himself invisible, he in a manner becomes visible to us in his works.

Correctly then is this world called the mirror of divinity; not that there is sufficient clearness for man to gain a full knowledge of God, by looking at the world, but that he has thus so far revealed himself, that the ignorance of the ungodly is without excuse. Now the faithful, to whom he has given eyes, see sparks of his glory, as it were, glittering in every created thing. The world was no doubt made, that it might be the theatre of the divine glory.[6]

R. KENT HUGHES

Sometimes I begin my personal time of prayer and devotion by reflecting on the mind-boggling size of the universe—that our own little galaxy has a hundred thousand million stars, that there are a hundred thousand million more galaxies each with a hundred thousand million stars, that our galaxy and each of those galaxies is a hundred light years across, and that there are three million light years between each of those galaxies. Absolutely phenomenal and amazing.

The opening line of the Old Testament says, "In the beginning God created the heavens and the earth" (Gen. 1:1). Now when it juxtaposes two words—*heavens* and *earth*—two opposites, it means he created everything. So you could really read that as, "In the beginning God created the cosmos." And then he said it was good, but he said even more than that. He said it was very good.

When we come to the New Testament and the fuller revelation of Jesus Christ, we learn that the cosmos is created by Christ himself. So the opening line of the Gospel of John says, "In the beginning was the word and the word was with God and the word was God. He was in the beginning with God, and without him was not anything made that was made." And so what we have there is the cosmic Christ, the Creator of all things. In fact, the apostle Paul brings both together in 1 Corinthians 8:6 when he says that our existence is due to the one God and Father and the one Lord Jesus Christ. All our existence depends on them.

And then you come to that incredible, lyrical song in Colossians 1:16–17, which speaks of Jesus: "For by him all things were created, in heaven and on earth, visible and invisible, whether thrones or dominions or rulers or authorities—all things were created through him and for him. And he is before all things, and in him all things hold together."

I've often thought that if I could commandeer the *Enterprise* from *Star Trek*, and I could travel out to our galaxy and across the Milky Way, and then kick it into warp speed eight so the galaxies would fly by like fence posts, and finally come to the very backwater of the universe, make a right turn and find a piece of stellar dust, it would have been created by Christ and sustained by Christ. Everything is made by Christ. The fires of Arcturus, the fires that light a firefly, all textures, all shapes, things in heaven, things on earth, things under the earth, things under the sea, everything is created and sustained by him.

And that means that, as he's the Creator of all things, everything is under his loving, benevolent care. We must also keep in mind that as human beings, the apex of creation, we were made in the image of God. But as regenerate people, we also have the image of Christ. Which means that we can rest in his goodness, in his great creation power, as he controls all of life, and we can flourish under him.

Prayer

Lord Who Spoke the World into Existence, we marvel at your creation, even though it has been corrupted. Your beauty is revealed in the splendor of the stars. Your might is shown forth in the strength of a hurricane. Your order is displayed in the laws of mathematics. Let everything that has breath praise the Lord for the works of his hands! Amen.

Question 6

How can we glorify God?

We glorify God by enjoying him, loving him, trusting him, and by obeying his will, commands, and law.

📖 **DEUTERONOMY 11:1**

You shall therefore love the LORD your God and keep his charge, his statutes, his rules, and his commandments always.

💬 **Commentary**

RICHARD SIBBES

As we receive all from God, so we should lay all at his feet, and say, "I will not live in a course of sin that will not stand with the favour of my God." . . .

True freedom is found when by the Spirit the heart is renewed, is enlarged, and becomes subordinate to God in Christ. A man is in a sweet frame when his heart is made subject to God, and drawn out towards him, for the God of all grace sets it at liberty. God will have us make his glory our aim, and then he will bestow grace and glory too upon us.[7]

BRYAN CHAPELL

How can we glorify God? We can do as he said, and we can believe what he said.

If you consider what it means to glorify God by doing what he said, then we have to remember what he said was the prime commandment, which was that we love him *above all* and that we walk with him *through all*. After all, the Lord Jesus said, "Love me with all your heart, soul, mind and strength. This is the first and the greatest commandment. The second is like unto it. Love you neighbor as yourself."

If we truly want to honor the Savior, we do as he said. But that means not just obeying him because he's going to get us. It's not really that. It's understanding how great is his love for us so that we, in love for him, want to walk with him. And that understanding means that we begin by saying, "I understand that he has loved me so much that my heart is responding in love for him."

As I do that, I'm not now honoring God with a sense of *Oh no, he's going to get me if I don't*. That would mean I might obey him, but I would not enjoy him. No, true love for God means I delight in his law. I understand that what God has given me when he says, "Walk with me," is a safe and good path in life. That's really what the commandments of God are about. They are explaining, as he shows us his character and care, that he's given us this safe path for life. If you get off the path, there are consequences, of course, because this is a safe and good path. But we are not staying on that path because we think somehow we are earning his affection. Rather, we understand, as he showed us through Christ and particularly the Lord's sacrifice for us, how great is his love for us. When we understand that the law or the commandments are echoing the character of God and his care for us, then we delight to walk in that path because it lets us experience the goodness of our God. That means, no matter what I face, I love God in all of life, and I want to walk with him through all of life. In that way I'm both honoring his heart—I glorify him because of how great is his love for me—and I show my love for him by walking in the path, not just out of drudgery, but actually with the sense of enjoying his goodness for my heart and life.

So many times people think they're glorifying God because they're just kind of bowing their necks and doing the awful thing they hate because otherwise God is going to hurt them. Or sometimes they do the things that they think God wants so that he'll give them more good stuff. But both those kinds of sanctified selfishness—I'm doing this so I will protect myself or promote myself—are not really love for God. When we understand that God gave his Son for me, that he's shown me his character and his care, then I understand that loving him and enjoying him means that I will delight to walk on that which provides the good and safe path for my life.

I'll walk with him and love him in all that he requires, because in doing so, I will actually enjoy the path that he has designed for the best life that he desires to give me.

✍ Prayer

Gracious Lord, we want to fully know and enjoy you. Open our eyes to see you as you are that we might trust you and long with all we are to keep your commands. Whether through small kindnesses or great courage, may each act of obedience bring you glory. Amen.

Question 7

What does the law of God require?

Personal, perfect, and perpetual obedience; that we love God with all our heart, soul, mind, and strength; and love our neighbor as ourselves. What God forbids should never be done and what God commands should always be done.

📖 MATTHEW 22:37–40

And [Jesus] said to him, "You shall love the Lord your God with all your heart and with all your soul and with all your mind. This is the great and first commandment. And a second is like it: You shall love your neighbor as yourself. On these two commandments depend all the Law and the Prophets."

💬 Commentary

JOHN WESLEY

Loving the Lord God with all your heart, mind, soul, and strength is the first great branch of Christian righteousness. You shall delight yourself in the Lord your God; seeking and finding all happiness in Him. You shall hear and fulfill His word, "My son, give me your heart." And having given Him your inmost soul to reign there without a rival, you may well cry out in the fulness of your heart, "I will love You, O my Lord, my strength. The Lord *is* my strong rock; my Savior, my God, in whom I trust." The second commandment, the second great branch of Christian righteousness, is closely and inseparably connected with the first: "Love your neighbor as yourself." Love—embrace with the most tender goodwill, the most earnest and cordial affection, the most inflamed desires of preventing or removing all evil and bringing every possible good. Your neighbor—not only your friends, kinfolk, or acquaintances; not only the virtuous ones who regard you, who extend or return your kindness, but every person, not excluding those you have never seen or know by name; not excluding those you know to be evil and unthankful, those who despitefully use you. Even those you shall love as yourself with the same invariable thirst after their happiness. Use the same unwearied care to screen them from whatever might grieve or hurt either their soul or body. This is love.[8]

JUAN SANCHEZ

When you ask, "What does the law of God require?" the short answer is *perfect obedience.* Now, that sounds daunting, but we have to understand the context in which the law was given. It was given in the context of grace, God's saving initiative. When God rescued Israel from Egypt and brought them to Sinai and declared, "If you obey my voice and keep my covenant," he essentially then said, "I will be your God and you will be my children." So the context of the law is God's saving initiative. The perfect obedience that the law demands is a response to God's saving initiative, and it is a wholehearted devotion.

The way that the Old Testament puts it is: "Love the LORD your God with all your heart and with all your soul and with all your might" (Deut. 6:5). The context of grace motivates a response of wholehearted devotion to the God who saves. It is a response of faith that is called love. And that love flows to love of neighbor as well.

There is only one problem. We cannot obey perfectly. But there is good news. In Jeremiah 31 God says that he will write the law on his people's hearts. In Ezekiel 36 God further explains: "I will remove the heart of stone from your flesh and give you a heart of flesh. And I will put my Spirit within you, and cause you to walk in my statutes" (vv. 26–27). These promises are linked to a new covenant that God would initiate through a promised king from David's line. The New Testament reveals that the promised King who inaugurates this new covenant is Jesus.

Jesus came to do what we ourselves could not do. While remaining fully God, Jesus came from heaven and took on our humanity in order to save us (Heb. 2:14–18). As our human representative, Jesus fulfilled the law of God by perfectly obeying God's commands and by paying the penalty of death that all lawbreakers owe. The gospel is an announcement that all who confess that they are guilty of breaking God's law and turn away from their sins and trust in Jesus have their sins forgiven and Jesus's perfect obedience accounted to them.

Through his life, death, burial, and resurrection, Jesus inaugurated the new covenant with its promises of a new heart (Jeremiah 31) and the indwelling of God's empowering Spirit (Ezekiel 36). Our only hope of fulfilling what the law requires is the new birth that was promised in the new covenant. Those who are born again to new life in Christ have been granted a new heart and God's indwelling Spirit, which empowers obedience.

The good news is that under the new covenant, God's people are empowered to obey God's law. Once again, we see that the commands of God don't *establish* a relationship with God. Obedience is our *response* to God's saving work. It is a loving response of faith. God has saved us in Jesus Christ, and we respond by trusting him in loving obedience.

✍ Prayer

Great Law-Giver, you have spoken a perfect law, and you deserve perfect obedience. Let us not merely think that your law requires outward submission; it demands the full assent of our minds and our hearts. Who is equal to such a task? We confess that we fall far short of keeping your law. Amen.

Question 8

What is the law of
God stated in the Ten
Commandments?

You shall have no other gods before me. You shall not make for yourself an idol in the form of anything in heaven above or on the earth beneath or in the waters below – you shall not bow down to them or worship them. You shall not misuse the name of the LORD your God. Remember the Sabbath day by keeping it holy. Honor your father and your mother. You shall not murder. You shall not commit adultery. You shall not steal. You shall not give false testimony. You shall not covet.

📖 EXODUS 20:3

You shall have no other gods before me.

💬 Commentary

JOHN BUNYAN

The danger doth not lie in the breaking of one or two of these ten only, but it doth lie even in the transgression of any one of them. As you know, if a king should give forth ten particular commands, to be obeyed by his subjects upon pain of death; now, if any man doth transgress against any one of these ten, he doth commit treason, as if he had broke them all, and lieth liable to have the sentence of the law as certainly passed on him, as if he had broken every particular of them. . . . These things are clear as touching the law of God, as it is a covenant of works: If a man do fulfill nine of the commandments, and yet breaketh but one, that being broken will as surely destroy him, and shut him out from the joys of heaven, as if he had actually transgressed against them all. . . . Though thou shouldst fulfill this covenant or law, even all of it, for a long time, ten, twenty, forty, fifty, or threescore years; yet if thou do chance to slip, and break one of them but once before thou die, thou art also gone and lost by that covenant. . . . As they that are under the covenant of grace shall surely be saved by it, so, even so, they that are under the covenants of works and the law, they shall surely be damned by it, if continuing therein.[9]

JOHN YATES

Because God created and loves us and knows what's best for us, he gives us moral and spiritual direction about how to live life in the best way. The Ten Commandments are a love gift to us from God. Of course this is true of all Scripture, but the heart and soul of God's guidance is found in the Ten Commandments. God spoke the words to Moses, and they were overheard by the children of Israel (Exodus 20). Later, Moses restated the Ten Commandments (Deuteronomy 5). The Ten Commandments are to be memorized, pondered, and committed to as a way of life.

Jesus taught and clarified the deeper meaning of the Ten Commandments for us. As he explained the Ten Commandments in the Gospels, he raised the bar on our understanding of what God expects of us. For instance, in Matthew 5:21, Jesus explained the meaning of the commandment not to murder. He said that actually anyone who is angry with his brother will be subject to judgment.

The first four commandments deal with our relationship with

God, and Jesus summarized them as: "You shall love the Lord your God with all your heart and with all your soul and with all your mind." The last six commandments address our relationship with our fellow man, and Jesus summarized them as: "Love your neighbor as yourself" (Matt. 22:37, 39).

The commandments are our treasure. We cherish them. They're a great gift, a love gift from God. They guide us. They warn us. They protect us. When we keep them, we show others what God is like. When we fail to live them, we bring great harm to ourselves and we dishonor our Maker.

We have a problem keeping the Ten Commandments because man is born in bondage to sin and selfishness. And in the end we cannot help but break God's holy law. But when we become a new creature by faith in Christ, we receive the indwelling Holy Spirit. We're freed from having to sin, and we're given the grace to keep God's law. Keeping God's commandments is not onerous but helps us live at peace with God, with ourselves, and with our neighbors.

We can learn to live out the Ten Commandments as we realize that they're God's gift to us. It's like learning to tell the truth. When you're young, you sometimes feel that you must protect yourself by deceiving others and not telling the truth. You learn as time goes not to deceive others. We learn to speak the truth. We learn to practice honesty.

That's why the prophets loved God's law and why we should, too. Keeping the Ten Commandments protects us. It protects society. These principles are at the heart of how God created us to live.

Prayer

Holy God, you showed your love to your people by giving them your commands. May we always give thanks for your law. You have not left us ignorant of how to walk in the way of righteousness. Help us to glorify you by obeying your Ten Commandments. Amen.

Question 9

What does God require in the first, second, and third commandments?

First, that we know and trust God as the only true and living God. Second, that we avoid all idolatry and do not worship God improperly. Third, that we treat God's name with fear and reverence, honoring also his Word and works.

📖 DEUTERONOMY 6:13–14

It is the LORD your God you shall fear. Him you shall serve and by his name you shall swear. You shall not go after other gods, the gods of the peoples who are around you.

💬 Commentary

CHARLES HADDON SPURGEON

God leads men to see that the God revealed in Scripture, and manifested in the person of the Lord Jesus, is the God who made heaven and earth. Man fashions for himself a god after his own liking; he makes to himself if not out of wood or stone, yet out of what he calls his own consciousness, or his cultured thought, a deity to his taste, who will not be too severe with his iniquities or deal out strict justice to the impenitent. He rejects God as he is, and elaborates other gods, such as he thinks the Divine One ought to be, and he says concerning these works of his own imagination, "These be thy gods, O Israel!"

The Holy Spirit, however, when he illuminates their minds, leads us to see that Jehovah is God, and beside him there is none else. He teaches his people to know that the God of heaven and earth is the God of the Bible, a God whose attributes are completely balanced, mercy attended by justice, love accompanied by holiness, grace arrayed in truth, and power linked with tenderness. He is not a God who winks at sin, much less is pleased with it, as the gods of the heathen are supposed to be, but a God who cannot look upon iniquity, and will by no means spare the guilty. This is the great quarrel of the present day between the philosopher and the Christian. The philosopher says, "Yes, a god if you will, but he must be of such a character as I now dogmatically set before you"; but the Christian replies, "Our business is not to invent a god, but to obey the one Lord who is revealed in the Scriptures of truth."[10]

JOHN LIN

The first three commandments show how we are to live in reference to and in light of the only true and living God.

The first commandment tells us that we are to have no other gods but God. He is to be the exclusive object of our worship, the ultimate object of our love and desire. The second commandment is similar and tells us that we are not to worship God according to our own conception of God, what the Bible calls *idolatry*. We must worship God according to who he is and not according to what we want him to be. In other words, do not worship false gods, and do not worship God falsely.

The third commandment is actually similar to the first two. We are not to misuse or mistreat the name of God. We know God's name describes his character, the essence of his being, which is why he told Moses that his name is "I AM." In other words, God is saying, "My name is that I'm self-existent and eternal." To not misuse the name of God doesn't merely mean that there are certain words we can or cannot say. It means that when we speak of God, whether through words or lifestyle, we are to fully honor and respect who he is.

Let's consider the first two commandments a bit more. Say, for instance, you believe in your heart that attaining some goal in your life—prestige, a certain kind of job, a relationship with the person of your dreams—will provide you with ultimate comfort and will answer your heart's desire for significance. In a daily functional way, you look to that goal to provide you with deeper comfort than God. That's breaking the first commandment. You've turned your goal into God. Prestige, a certain job, or a person has become the object of your worship.

The flip side is that if you worship God because you believe that he should provide you with comfort by providing the prestige, the job, or the relationship that you desire and are looking for, you are also violating the commandments. You've imposed your conception of who God is on God. You've created a custom designer god, an idol. These first two commandments are that we worship God alone, that we worship God as a true God, and that we not worship a designer god or an idol.

So why do these commandments insist on us worshiping God alone and worshiping God as he is and not as we want him to be? Why is the third commandment so insistent on honoring and respecting his name and his character? It is because God created us with a desire that only he can fulfill—a desire for him. If we are always trying to change who God is or replace him with something else, we'll never be at peace. We'll never experience true comfort, true significance, or true joy. We'll never be whole. But if God is at the center of our lives, not another god or a revised version of God, but the true and living God, we'll truly be at peace.

This is precisely why Augustine wrote, "You've made us for yourself, and our heart is restless until it rests in you."[11]

🖐 Prayer

One and Only God, your name is above all names, and we come before you in reverence and fear. Keep us true to your commandments. Reveal to us any false gods in our lives. Let us worship you alone in spirit and truth. Amen.

What does God require in the fourth and fifth commandments?

Fourth, that on the Sabbath day we spend time in public and private worship of God, rest from routine employment, serve the Lord and others, and so anticipate the eternal Sabbath. Fifth, that we love and honor our father and our mother, submitting to their godly discipline and direction.

📖 LEVITICUS 19:3

Every one of you shall revere his mother and his father, and you shall keep my Sabbaths: I am the LORD your God.

💬 Commentary

JOHN CALVIN

It is now easy to understand the doctrine of the law—viz. that God, as our Creator, is entitled to be regarded by us as a Father and Master, and should, accordingly, receive from us fear, love, reverence, and glory; nay, that we are not our own, to follow whatever course passion dictates, but are bound to obey him implicitly, and to acquiesce entirely in his good pleasure. Again, the Law teaches, that justice and rectitude are a delight, injustice an abomination to him, and, therefore, as we would not with impious ingratitude revolt from our Maker, our whole life must be spent in the cultivation of righteousness. For if we manifest becoming reverence only when we prefer his will to our own, it follows, that the only legitimate service to him is the practice of justice, purity, and holiness. Nor can we plead as an excuse, that we want the power, and, like debtors, whose means are exhausted, are unable to pay. We cannot be permitted to measure the glory of God by our ability; whatever we may be, he ever remains like himself, the friend of righteousness, the enemy of unrighteousness, and whatever his demands from us may be, as he can only require what is right, we are necessarily under a natural obligation to obey.[12]

TIMOTHY KELLER

If we read the entire Bible, Old and New Testaments, we come to see that the command to remember the Sabbath day has two aspects to it.

First, it's a crucial practice. In our lives we're commanded to have a rhythm of work and rest, and we are forbidden to overwork.

We're also commanded to nurture our bodies and our souls. We're not supposed to nurture only our bodies. We're to rejuvenate our souls through fellowship and through prayer and devotion and worship every week.

It's also true, however, that the New Testament shows us that the Sabbath day points to a deeper kind of rest. Hebrews 4 in particular says that when we believe in Christ and the gospel, we rest from our works. Which means the great burden of having to prove ourselves and having to earn our salvation is lifted from us. In this life we get much of that deeper rest, and yet it's only completely realized in the future in the new heavens and new earth. And we look for that and we long for that. It's deeply consoling especially at times in which we're very weary.

The fifth commandment to honor our parents should also be read in light of the gospel. The command says that as children, we should obey our parents. As adults, we should respect and listen to our parents. And yet the gospel also reminds us that God is our Father, by grace we're brought into his family, and he is our primary source of love. And if our primary *phileo* relationship is with him, then we are able to love and honor our parents well, not looking to them to provide what can be found in God alone.

✋ Prayer

Life-Giving Father, we will flourish only when we walk in your ways. You have made us, and you tell us we need rest. Keep us from justifying ourselves through ceaseless work. Give us humility to honor our parents. May we always live by your commands rather than by our own instincts. Amen.

What does God require in the sixth, seventh, and eighth commandments?

Sixth, that we do not hurt, or hate, or be hostile to our neighbor, but be patient and peaceful, pursuing even our enemies with love. Seventh, that we abstain from sexual immorality and live purely and faithfully, whether in marriage or in single life, avoiding all impure actions, looks, words, thoughts, or desires, and whatever might lead to them. Eighth, that we do not take without permission that which belongs to someone else, nor withhold any good from someone we might benefit.

📖 ROMANS 13:9

For the commandments, "You shall not commit adultery, You shall not murder, You shall not steal, You shall not covet," and any other commandment, are summed up in this word: "You shall love your neighbor as yourself."

🗩 Commentary

MARTYN LLOYD-JONES

Man cannot even keep the Ten Commandments. And yet he talks glibly about keeping the Sermon on the Mount, and of imitating Christ. . . . And if a man cannot keep the Ten Commandments, as they understand them, what hope have they of keeping the Ten Commandments as they have been interpreted by the Lord Jesus Christ? That was the whole trouble with the Pharisees, who so hated him and who finally crucified him. They thought they were keeping the Ten Commandments and the moral law. Our Lord convinced them and convicted them of the fact that they were not doing so. They claimed that they had never committed murder. Wait a minute, said our Lord. Have you ever said to your brother, "Thou fool"? If you have, you are guilty of murder. Murder does not only mean actually, physically, killing a man, it means that bitterness and hatred in your heart. . . . And he taught the same, you remember, with regard to adultery. They claimed that they were guiltless. But wait a minute, says our Lord, you say you have never committed adultery? "But I say unto you, that whosoever looketh on a woman to lust after her, hath committed adultery with her already in his heart" (Matt. 5:28). He is guilty; he has coveted, he has desired. You see, as our Lord comes to interpret the law, he shows that an evil desire is as damnable as a deed. A thought and an imagination are as reprehensible in the sight of God as the act committed.[13]

STEPHEN UM

Christians are obligated to obey the Ten Commandments, because what we find in the Ten Commandments are the laws of God. What we find in Jesus's interpretation in the Sermon on the Mount is that the standards of the law are much higher than we had assumed. It's not just not committing adultery and not murdering and not stealing. Jesus says, in interpreting the sixth commandment, that if you harbor bitterness, if you're unable to forgive someone, if you call a person *raca* (that is, to consider him a nonperson), then you've murdered that person in your heart. He also says that if you lust in your heart, you're breaking the seventh commandment and committing adultery. And you are being greedy if you're materialistic and you're not radically generous. So Jesus raises the bar of the commandments to the highest level.

Martin Luther wrote that you cannot break the rest of the commandments without first breaking the first one.[14] That is, if you break the commandments, you are looking at other things as your ultimate value and your god rather than God himself.

Luther also said that when there is a negative prohibition in the Ten Commandments, a positive implication is assumed.[15] Therefore, when it says that you ought not to murder, it also means that you ought to radically love others, even neighbors and enemies. And when it says you ought not to commit adultery, the assumption is that you're supposed to be faithful to your wife or to your husband and to recognize sexuality as a beautiful gift from God. And therefore if you're in a marriage relationship, you ought to recognize that it is a covenantal commitment between a man and a woman. When it says that you ought not to steal, the understanding is that you ought to be radically generous.

These are the responsibilities that Christians have in responding to the Ten Commandments. But the problem is that we're unable to obey them perfectly. So how are we going to resolve that tension?

Jesus Christ is the second Adam, the true Israel, the individual divine corporate head and representative who has come to fulfill the obligations of the law perfectly in himself. His obedience and righteousness now gets imputed into our lives, thereby giving us the ability to obey the obligations and the demands of the law. Even when we don't obey them perfectly, we know that we are not going to be crushed by the law, and we will have confidence as we seek to obey the law of God because we know that Jesus Christ has fulfilled those requirements perfectly for us. Therefore, we can live without fear of rejection from God for our disobedience or lack of perfect obedience. But we know that Jesus Christ has accomplished all these things, fulfilling the requirements of the law perfectly for us.

Prayer

Faithful Shepherd of Our Souls, you created us to live in love and fellowship on the earth, but we fail in that again and again. May your love rule every relationship so that we walk in purity, putting away lust, covetousness, and greed, for your name's sake. Amen.

Question 12

What does God require
in the ninth and tenth
commandments?

Ninth, that we do not lie or deceive, but speak the truth in love. Tenth,
that we are content, not envying anyone or resenting what God has
given them or us.

📖 JAMES 2:8

If you really fulfill the royal law according to the Scripture, "You shall
love your neighbor as yourself," you are doing well.

🗨 Commentary

JOHN BRADFORD

Thou Shalt Not Bear False Witness Against Thy Neighbour. Now
dost thou, most gracious Lord, instruct me in this commandment,
how I should use my tongue towards my neighbour, and behave myself concerning his name, forbidding me to bear false witness; in the
which thou forbiddest me all kinds of slandering, lying, hypocrisy,

and untruth. And why? Because, as "members of one body," thou wouldest we should "speak truth one to another," and be careful every one to cover others' infirmity, and with our tongue defend the names of others, even as we would that others should defend ours: so that in this commandment, as thou forbiddest me all kind of evil, perilous, calumnious and untrue speaking, so dost thou command to me all kind of godly, honest, and true report and talk. . . . O how great a good thing is this unto me! If we consider the hurt that cometh by untruth, and by words wherethrough many are deceived, easily may we see a wonderful benefit and care of thee for us in this commandment.

Thou Shalt Not Covet. . . . Here, O most gracious Lord God, thou givest me the last commandment of thy law who having taught me what outward actions I shall avoid, that I do not thereby offend or undo my neighbour, as murder, adultery, theft, and false witness, *now* thou teachest me a rule for my heart, to order that well, from the abundance whereof all our works and words proceed, that I shall not covet any thing that is my neighbour's. I know hereby that, if he have a fairer house than I, I may not wish for it; if he have a more beautiful wife than I, I may not desire her. . . . I may not desire to take from him his ox, nor his ass, no, not his dog, no, not the meanest thing he hath in his possession. So that, in the other commandments as thou hast forbidden all injuries and evil practice against my neighbour, so now thou chargest me to beware of thinking any evil thought against him. . . . The apostle said well, when he taught us, saying, "Cast all your care upon God, for he careth for you." It is true, I find it true: thus thou "carest for us," and wouldest have us to "care one for another."[16]

THABITI ANYABWILE

The tongue is a restless evil. It sets the whole person on fire, James 3 tells us. And so the ninth commandment is aimed in part at bridling the tongue. It's aimed at bridling the tongue with truth, teaching us to put off falsehood, to put off lying. In our culture, to accuse someone of telling a *lie* is a serious insult, so many people hesitate to even use the term. I think that this hesitancy reveals fallen man's heart to shy away from this commandment—as well as his need of this commandment.

What does it mean that we think the command "thou shalt not lie" or the word *lie* is impolite? It probably indicates that in some ways we're already shading the truth. We're already pulling back from a full expression of what's good, what's right, and what's true. And the ninth commandment convicts us of that. It points out our fallenness when it comes to our use of the tongue and the destruction that the tongue represents.

And, likewise, the tenth commandment: "Thou shalt not covet." If you can imagine the heart having hands, coveting is like the heart grasping for things, desiring things, laying hold of things that don't properly belong to it. What's remarkable and beautiful about this commandment—about all of Scripture, in fact—is that even though the commandment addresses something inward (that inward grasping of the heart), it also points out the social implications of that interior grasping. So we have "thou shalt not covet anything *that is thy neighbor's.*" Not our neighbor's spouse, not our neighbor's cattle, not anything that belongs to our neighbor.

The tenth commandment sets for us a kind of boundary that protects against the way covetousness tends to cross lines. We are tempted to cross the line of desires, longing for things that aren't properly in our possession. We cross the line of property, grasping for things that belong to another person (your neighbor's cattle, your neighbor's spouse). So our coveting actually, socially, does injury to our neighbor. And there's another line that we cross. When we covet, what we're actually saying is that God has not apportioned his creation properly because he hasn't given us everything we desire. And so the heart, in its fallen, sinful way, grasps for things that don't belong to it and seeks for things that actually belong on the other side of ownership—to the neighbor or to God.

These commandments speak to us, and they call us forth to truth-telling. And not just to truth-telling, but to the truth spoken *in love.*

They call forth a bridling, a restraining, and a channeling of desire to things that are good and right. They call us to things that God has legitimately given to us for our enjoyment, and to be content in how God has distributed his blessing, how he rules his creation. They call us not to go outside of that contentment by taking things, for if we do, we destroy society, culture, and our neighbors. This is true even if the taking of what doesn't belong to us is only a taking in heart.

Prayer

Lord of All Truth, help us to reflect your goodness in word and deed. You know all things. Nothing is hidden from you. You give good gifts and withhold no good thing from your children. May your truth be on our lips and contentment be in our hearts. Amen.

Can anyone keep the law of God perfectly?

Since the fall, no mere human has been able to keep the law of God perfectly, but consistently breaks it in thought, word, and deed.

📖 ROMANS 3:10–12

> None is righteous, no, not one;
>> no one understands;
>> no one seeks for God.
> All have turned aside; together they have become worthless;
>> no one does good,
>> not even one.

💬 Commentary

JOHN OWEN

As a traveler, in his way meeting with a violent storm of thunder and rain, immediately turns out of his way to some house or tree for his shelter; but yet this causeth him not to give over his journey; so soon as the storm is over he returns to his way and progress again. So it is with men in bondage to sin: the law meets with them in a storm of thunder and lightning from heaven, terrifies and hinders them in their way; this turns them for a season out of their course; they will run to prayer or amendment of life, for some shelter from the storm of wrath which is feared coming upon their consciences. But is their course stopped? Are their principles altered? Not at all; so soon as the storm is over . . . they return to their former course, in the service of sin again.[17]

Never let us reckon that our work in contending against sin, in crucifying, mortifying, and subduing of it, is at an end. The place of its habitation is unsearchable; and when we may think that we have thoroughly won the field, there is still some reserve remaining that we saw not, that we knew not of. Many conquerors have been ruined by their carelessness after a victory; and many have been spiritually wounded after great successes against this enemy. . . . There is no way for us to pursue sin in its unsearchable habitation but by being endless in our pursuit.[18]

LEO SCHUSTER

God created us to love, enjoy, glorify, and obey him, and in so doing, flourish as human beings. Why then do we struggle so much to do that? Like an incredibly sophisticated piece of machinery that's broken, we don't operate the way we were designed to because of the fall. What's the fall? God created humans with the capacity to keep his law perfectly, but that was lost when the first human and representative of the human race, Adam, chose to rebel and disobey God. He fell into a condition of sin and dragged all of us with him. The Bible describes that condition in a variety of ways—spiritual rebellion, blindness, illness, bondage, and death.

How does it affect us today? As a result of the fall we're not just spiritually impaired but incapacitated. We're not just weak; we have no innate power to obey God's law and glorify him. We're estranged from our Creator, from one another, and from the rest of creation. In this spiritually disabled condition, we're unable to obey God's law not only in our actions and words, but even in our thoughts, attitudes, and motivations. As the prophet Jeremiah put it, "The heart is deceitful above all things, and desperately sick; who can understand it?" (17:19). And so we stand alienated and guilty before the holy God of heaven and earth.

That's very discouraging, of course, to contemplate, but it's not the end of the story; it's just the beginning. It's the bad news that stands as the backdrop for the spectacularly good news of the gospel, which brings life and hope. Though we're unable to keep the law of God perfectly, there is One who kept the law perfectly for us. Jesus faithfully obeyed his Father, even to the point of death on the cross, so that we who trust alone in him might no longer live under the guilt, power, and bondage of sin but be set free. Jesus said, "So if the Son sets you free, you will be free indeed" (John 8:36). And though we fell in Adam, we have been raised with Christ. We're confident that the God who raised Jesus from the dead is lovingly at work in us and won't let us go until the day when he will bring us into his everlasting presence in glory where we will no longer struggle. There we will finally, fully, and freely obey the One who made us and redeemed us.

🖐 Prayer

Holy God, left to our own devices, we transgress your law at every turn. We have no defense, but must plead guilty before your throne of judgment. Your law condemns us and cuts through our pretensions to righteousness, convincing us that we desperately need a Savior. Amen.

Question 14

Did God create us unable to keep his law?

No, but because of the disobedience of our first parents, Adam and Eve, all of creation is fallen; we are all born in sin and guilt, corrupt in our nature and unable to keep God's law.

📖 ROMANS 5:12

Therefore, just as sin came into the world through one man, and death through sin, and so death spread to all men because all sinned.

💬 Commentary

ABRAHAM BOOTH

I believe, that in the beginning God created the heavens and the earth, with all their numerous inhabitants. Last of all, and nobly conspicuous amongst the amazingly diversified productions of his almighty power and infinite skill . . . he created man, and constituted him lord of this lower world. Male and female created he them, after his own image and in his own likeness: upright, innocent, and holy; capable of serving and glorifying their bountiful Creator.

On the same warrant, I believe, that man did not long continue in these holy and happy circumstances; but, being left to the freedom of his own will, he transgressed the law which his Maker and Sovereign had given him; in consequence of which he fell into a state of guilt, depravity, and ruin. And as he was not only the natural but federal head and representative of his unborn posterity, he sinning, all his offspring sinned in him and fell with him, the guilt of his first sin being imputed, and a corrupt nature derived, to all who descend from him by natural generation. Hence it is that all men are by nature the children of wrath; averse to all that is spiritually good, and prone to evil; dead in sin, under the curse of the righteous law and obnoxious to eternal vengeance. From which state of complicated misery there is no deliverance but by Jesus Christ, the second Adam.[19]

DAVID BISGROVE

Being a parent is a wide-open window into the human condition. For example, I'm constantly having to remind and encourage and cajole my young children to say "please" and "thank you" and to share. But I never have to encourage them to say "mine!" or to grab things that don't belong to them or to hoard toys from one another.

Now where does this self-centered impulse come from? The Bible is helpful here because it gives us a vocabulary to talk about why we seem to be born with this self-centered disposition. You see, we're told that when God created Adam and Eve, he created them in his image. That means, among other things, that they reflected his goodness. God affirmed their goodness when he looked at his creation, including Adam and Eve, and said, "It is very good." So Adam and Eve had a perfect relationship with God. They were able to love and obey him perfectly. But then we're told that Satan tempted them with a lie that God isn't good, that he can't be trusted, that real freedom is found apart from God and his law. And so when Adam believed and acted on that lie, Paul tells us in Romans 5, sin entered the world the way a virus enters the body, infecting all mankind from that time on.

This is why from my earliest days, and my children's earliest days, and, in the future, their children's earliest days, we all say, "Mine."

Now this doesn't mean that people are devoid of all goodness. We're made in God's image and therefore we're still capable of doing good and beautiful things. But sin has corrupted our ability to love and obey God with our whole hearts, strength, and minds. Sin has infected every part of us, so that we're all born in sin and guilt, corrupt in our nature, and unable to keep God's law.

Consider one example. Imagine a hungry lion, and imagine putting two plates of food in front of him—one a plate of raw red meat, the other a plate of perfectly cooked string beans. The lion can choose either one, but because of his nature he's always going to choose the red meat.

See, when Adam sinned as our representative, our nature became enslaved to sin so that we no longer want or seek God. But when Christ came, he was the second Adam, and where the first Adam failed, the second Adam succeeded. Where the first Adam brought death through his disobedience and selfishness, the second Adam, Jesus Christ, brought life through his obedience and sacrifice on the cross.

✋ Prayer

Merciful Lord, we are corrupt in our very natures. We are sons and daughters of the first Adam who desire what you forbid. Give us a new nature through new birth in Christ, the second Adam, that we might be able to keep your law in the power of the Holy Spirit. Amen.

Question 15

Since no one can keep the law, what is its purpose?

That we may know the holy nature and will of God, and the sinful nature and disobedience of our hearts; and thus our need of a Savior. The law also teaches and exhorts us to live a life worthy of our Savior.

📖 ROMANS 3:20

For by works of the law no human being will be justified in his sight, since through the law comes knowledge of sin.

💬 Commentary

CHARLES SIMEON

These poor men think they can preach the Gospel without preaching the Law. I say, they must preach the Law, unless they do not mean to preach the Gospel. The Law entered that the offence might abound: proclaim it, I say, for this purpose among your ungodly congregations; lift up your voices like trumpets, and tell the people their transgressions, that you may glorify the more your honoured Master, in proclaiming the infinite riches and fulness of His great salvation. Preach the Law to those who believe, as finished, cancelled, dead for their salvation: point them to Immanuel as holding it in His bleeding hand, and saying to them, "If ye love me, keep my Commandments."[20]

LIGON DUNCAN

The law of God helps us to know God, know ourselves, know our need, and know the life of peace and blessedness. It helps us to know God because it specifically reveals his character and his attributes, his holy will, what he's like.

Paul tells us in Romans 1 that everyone knows right and wrong. But the law of God very specifically reveals to us God's character and his own moral qualities. Morality is not arbitrary. God doesn't tell us to do arbitrary things. God does not require us to do things that he is not prepared to do himself. So all morality is rooted in God's character. And when we study the law, we see a display of God's character.

God's law also reveals to us ourselves, especially our sinful nature and our disobedience, our inclination to sin. For instance, when Jesus is talking to the rich young ruler, he says, "Go, sell what you possess, and give to the poor" (Matt. 19:21). And the rich young ruler essentially says to Jesus, "I can't." And he walks away sadly. Now what's going on in that story? Is Jesus saying that we all have to give away all of our possessions? No. But in the case of the rich young ruler, Jesus is revealing to him by the law of God the specific nature of his own sin. What's the first commandment? To have no other gods before me. And there, God in the flesh is saying to the rich young ruler, "What's it going to be? Your money, your possessions, or me, God?" And the rich young ruler chooses something over God, before God.

That leads to the third thing that the law helps us with. It helps us to understand our need. When we know who God is, and we know that we don't measure up to his morality and character, when we know who we are, and we know the sinful inclinations of our hearts, it presses us to Jesus, because we know that we have need of a Savior. And the Savior has fulfilled that law. He's obeyed it perfectly, and he's paid the penalty that is due to us for it. The law presses us to the Savior. It points us to the Savior. It takes us to the Savior.

Of course, the law also shows us the life of peace and blessedness. When we think about obedience, many of us immediately think, "Oh, do I have to? Do I have to do good works? Do I have to obey?" That wasn't Jesus's attitude toward God's commands and God's will. In fact, he frequently said to his disciples, "My food is to do the will of him who sent me" (John 4:34). In other words, he was saying that it was like spreading a seven-course banquet in front of him to be able to obey the law of God, the will of God. And once we're redeemed, once we've trusted in Jesus Christ alone for salvation as he has offered in the gospel, the law not only is something that points us to Christ, but it also shows us how to live the life of peace and blessedness.

When God originally gave his commands to Adam and Eve in the garden, he gave those commands to them as blessings. They weren't things upon which his love was contingent. He loved them and blessed them in the garden. And their obedience to the commands was the very sphere in which they enjoyed that blessedness. And when we are saved by Christ, when we are united to Christ, we are able to walk in a manner that is worthy of the gospel. We are to live in a manner that is like the Lord Jesus Christ. And he delighted in obeying God. And so the law of God shows us what that life of peace and blessedness is like. It shows us what it's like to live a life worthy of the gospel once we've trusted in Jesus Christ.

Prayer

Giver of All Good Gifts, your law reveals to us what is just. Though it condemns us, through it we know how great is your holiness and how perfect is your Son. Though we fall short, may we always give you thanks and praise for your law and rejoice that we have a Savior. Amen.

Question 16

What is sin?

Sin is rejecting or ignoring God in the world he created, rebelling against him by living without reference to him, not being or doing what he requires in his law – resulting in our death and the disintegration of all creation.

📖 1 JOHN 3:4

Everyone who makes a practice of sinning also practices lawlessness; sin is lawlessness.

💬 Commentary

OSWALD CHAMBERS

Sin is a fundamental relationship; it is not wrong doing, it is wrong *being*, deliberate and emphatic independence of God. The Christian religion bases everything on the positive, radical nature of sin. Other religions deal with sins; the Bible alone deals with sin. The first thing Jesus Christ faced in men was the heredity of sin, and it is because we have ignored this in our presentation of the Gospel that the message of the Gospel has lost its sting and its blasting power.[21]

JOHN LIN

One very important way of understanding sin is that sin is rebellion against God's law. It's not doing what he requires of us, not living as he has called us to live, and, therefore, never fully being who God created us to be. Sin is living without reference to God, not viewing him to be the defining reality of our lives around which our entire lives need to be centered. And when we don't live as if God is who he is, we violate his law and all the good, loving, protecting guidelines that he's provided to us for how to best and most fully live.

Think about it this way. If you were to walk off a cliff saying, "I don't have to live by the law of gravity; I can live by my own rules," you would, on the one hand, be disobeying a very specific rule and commandment—namely, "Don't walk off a cliff." But on the other hand, you would also not be living in reference to gravity. You would be living as if gravity were of no consequence or importance in your life. You would never say the law of gravity is arbitrary, or that it is unreasonable that you have to obey it. You would never say that, because you understand that gravity is something that we must live in reference to. Of course there are guidelines to honor and boundaries to acknowledge. You know the result of walking off a cliff and trying to break the law of gravity: death and disintegration.

When we don't live as if God is God, when we break God's loving law, when we fail to honor who he is, when we say or imply by our actions that he's of no consequence or importance in this or that part of our lives, we fail to fully be the people God created us to be. And it leads to death and disintegration.

This illustration might help. Our solar system exists harmoniously when all the planets orbit the same center: the sun. If, however, the planets all decided on their own what to orbit, or if some of the planets chose not to orbit anything, what would happen? Death and disintegration. The solar system as we know it would unravel and fall apart because the planets would not be orbiting the correct center. They wouldn't be living in reference to the sun. And therefore everything would fall apart and be destroyed.

Not living in reference to God not only leads to our personal death and disintegration; it's the reason why the entire cosmos is subject to death and disintegration. God created Adam and Eve to be the centerpiece and the pinnacle of creation. When they sinned, their disobedience of God's loving law not only had implications on their lives, it also had implications on the entire cosmos.

Paul writes that "the wages of sin is death" (Rom. 6:23). Sin leads to death. And yet the gospel is that Jesus Christ experienced death so that we could live. In some ways he was disintegrated on the cross, spiritually torn apart, so that we could be made whole. He died for our sin, so that we could be made alive. He experienced death and disintegration. He paid the penalty for our sin, so that we would not have to.

Prayer

Lord of the Universe, all your ways are good. We pursue the way of death when we go our own way. Help us to see sin as the poison it is. Let your law, rather than the spirit of lawlessness, shape our minds and our lives. Amen.

Question 17

What is idolatry?

Idolatry is trusting in created things rather than the Creator for our hope and happiness, significance and security.

📖 ROMANS 1:21 AND 25

For although they knew God, they did not honor him as God or give thanks to him, but they became futile in their thinking, and their foolish hearts were darkened. . . . They exchanged the truth about God for a lie and worshiped and served the creature rather than the Creator. . . .

💬 Commentary

MARTIN LUTHER

What is it to have a god? Or, what is one's god? Answer: To whatever we look for any good thing and for refuge in every need, that is what is meant by "god." . . . Many a person imagines that he has God and everything he needs, provided he has money and property. . . . The evidence for this appears when people are arrogant, secure, and proud because of such possessions, but desperate when they lack them or lose them. I repeat, to have a god means to have something on which one's heart depends entirely.

Question and explore your own heart thoroughly, and you will find out if it embraces God alone or not. Do you have it in your heart to expect nothing but good things from God, especially when you are in trouble and in need? And does your heart in addition give up and forsake everything that is not God? Then you have the one true God. On the other hand, is your heart attached to and does it rely on something else, from which you hope to receive more good and more help than from God? And when things go wrong, do you, instead of fleeing to Him, flee from Him? Then you have another god, a false god, an idol.[22]

TIMOTHY KELLER

The last catechism answer showed us that sin is rejecting, ignoring, and rebelling against God, not treating God as God, and not giving him the honor that is his due. In the Bible, the most frequently described way that human beings do that is through the sin of idolatry. Idolatry is loving anything more than Jesus Christ. Idolatry is treating anything as more important than Jesus Christ for your meaning in life, for your happiness, for your security and hope, or for your self-regard. The reason why it's so important to understand the sin of idolatry is that it can be growing in a part of your life for a long time and get very deep without it right away leading to clear, visible, and easily seen violations of God's law.

So, for example, if affluence and your career have become too important to you, they've become idols, and that can lead you to working too hard and exhaustion. It can lead you to becoming ruthless. It can block the development of a loving heart and the fruit of the Spirit. It can thin out your relationships. It can hurt your family relationships. It can hurt your friendships. And all these things can be going on for a long time before it leads to a real overt example of lying or cheating or adultery, because idolatry can lead to those things.

So what's important to grasp is this: sin is not just doing bad things. It's turning good things into ultimate things, because it ruins your soul, destroys community, and dishonors God.

🖐 Prayer

Creator God, forgive us for worshiping the things you have made. No person or thing should be our hope or our trust. You alone are self-existent and all sufficient. May you be our all in all. Amen.

Question 18

Will God allow our disobedience and idolatry to go unpunished?

No, every sin is against the sovereignty, holiness, and goodness of God, and against his righteous law, and God is righteously angry with our sins and will punish them in his just judgment both in this life, and in the life to come.

📖 EPHESIANS 5:5–6

For you may be sure of this, that everyone who is sexually immoral or impure, or who is covetous (that is, an idolater), has no inheritance in the kingdom of Christ and God. Let no one deceive you with empty words, for because of these things the wrath of God comes upon the sons of disobedience.

💬 Commentary

CHARLES HADDON SPURGEON

Not to punish the guilty were to exact the penalty of suffering from the innocent. Think what an injury and injustice would be inflicted upon all the honest men in London if the thieves were never punished for their roguery. It would be making the innocent suffer if you allowed the guilty to escape. God, therefore, not out of arbitrary choice, but from very necessity of rightness, must punish us for having done wrong.[23]

ALISTAIR BEGG

When Paul preached before Felix and Drusilla, he essentially had three points—righteousness, self-control, and the judgment to come (Acts 24). The fact that Felix and Drusilla were in an adulterous relationship did not prevent Paul from speaking very clearly about the justice of God. It was, if you like, almost a hallmark of his preaching. At the end of his address in Athens he says the same thing: "[God] has fixed a day on which he will judge the world" (Acts 17:31). The Bible makes it clear that we won't escape detection or conviction or sentence forever. There is going to be a payday.

The idea that God is too kind ever to condemn sin and that everyone in the end will go to heaven does not actually find a basis in the Bible itself. Paul's warning in Ephesians 5 is to those who have professed faith in Jesus, so that they will not pay attention to those who suggest other than what he's teaching them, namely, that this day will come—a day that is fixed, a day that will be absolutely fair, and a day when the judgment rendered will be absolutely final.

Prayer

Righteous Lord, if we think that we are good, we deceive ourselves. We deserve your wrath. We have broken your commands, and we have not loved you with our whole hearts, minds, and strength. We can only plead the righteousness of Christ and ask you to let our punishment fall on him. Amen.

Question 19

Is there any way to escape punishment and be brought back into God's favor?

Yes, to satisfy his justice, God himself, out of mere mercy, reconciles us to himself and delivers us from sin and from the punishment for sin, by a Redeemer.

📖 ISAIAH 53:10–11

> Yet it was the will of the LORD to crush him;
>   he has put him to grief;
> when his soul makes an offering for guilt,
>   he shall see his offspring; he shall prolong his days;
> the will of the LORD shall prosper in his hand.
> Out of the anguish of his soul he shall see and be satisfied;
> by his knowledge shall the righteous one, my servant,
>   make many to be accounted righteous,
>   and he shall bear their iniquities.

⊟ Commentary

JONATHAN EDWARDS

But is there any thing which Christians can find in heaven or earth, so worthy to be the objects of their admiration and love, their earnest and longing desires, their hope and their rejoicing, and their fervent zeal, as those things that are held forth to us in the gospel of Jesus Christ? In which not only are things declared most worthy to affect us, but they are exhibited in the most affecting manner. The glory and beauty of the blessed Jehovah, which is most worthy in itself to be the object of our admiration and love, is there exhibited in the most affecting manner that can be conceived of, as it appears, shining in all its lustre, in the face of an incarnate, infinitely loving, meek, compassionate, dying Redeemer. All the virtues of the Lamb of God, his humility, patience, meekness, submission, obedience, love and compassion, are exhibited to our view in a manner the most tending to move our affections of any that can be imagined; as they all had their greatest trial, and their highest exercise, and so their brightest manifestation, when he was in the most affecting circumstances; even when he was under his last sufferings, those unutterable and unparalleled sufferings he endured from his tender love and pity to us. There also, the hateful nature of our sins is manifested in the most affecting manner possible; as we see the dreadful effects of them in what our Redeemer, who undertook to answer for us, suffered for them. And there we have the most affecting manifestation of God's hatred of sin, and his wrath and justice in punishing it; as we see his justice in the strictness and inflexibleness of it, and his wrath in its terribleness, in so dreadfully punishing our sins, in one, who was infinitely dear to him and loving to us. So has God disposed things in the affair of our redemption, and in his glorious dispensations, revealed to us in the gospel, as though every thing were purposely contrived in such a manner as to have the greatest possible tendency to reach our hearts in the most tender part, and move our affections most sensibly and strongly. How great cause have we therefore to be humbled to the dust that we are no more affected![24]

MIKA EDMONDSON

The movie theater experience just isn't the same without the lights off. I learned this firsthand when, after the first thirty seconds of *Star Wars: The Force Awakens* accidently played in a lit theater, three irritated guys stormed out and demanded that the staff turn the lights down. A dark backdrop contrasted against a light image adds volume and drama to the total experience.

We might say that the catechism is set up that way as well. God's just and righteous judgment against our sin provides the dark backdrop against which the glory of the gospel shines through. After we've understood the depth of our calamity, we can better appreciate the true magnitude of God's rescue plan for us.

The catechism tells us that God freely and mercifully satisfied the demands of his own justice on our behalf. According to Isaiah 53, God made the righteous life of his servant (Jesus Christ) to be a substitutionary offering for the unrighteous. In obedience to God's will, Jesus Christ lived the life we should have lived and so fulfilled the just requirements of God's law on our behalf. Yet he also died the death we should have died. Isaiah's graphic language of the servant being "crushed" and "put to grief" (Isa. 53:10) reminds us of the heavy price of our sin. At the cross, Jesus bore the full weight of God's curse against sin and so fully satisfied the demands of God's just condemnation against sin. So we have a righteous life that satisfies the justice of God for us and an atoning death that satisfies the justice of God for us. This great exchange is the heart of the gospel itself.

Perhaps the most startling aspect of Isaiah's language is that it "pleased" the Lord to make this exchange. Somehow, it actually pleased the Lord to hand his innocent Son over to be mocked, brutalized, and crucified. That's a nearly impossible truth to fathom until you realize why God was pleased by this. Certainly, God was not pleased by the sin of Judas who betrayed Jesus, the religious leaders who hated him, Pilate who unjustly sentenced him, or the misguided crowd who rejected him. But God was pleased by the active and passive (through suffering) obedience of his Son, who continued to trust

God and love his people no matter the cost. God was pleased to lay his judgment upon the Son in order to save his sinful people. God was pleased because, through the cross, the Son of God would be glorified, the people of God would be saved, the justice of God would be satisfied, and the love of God would be revealed. The cross was not a tragic accident. It was God's will, his plan to save his people through the work of the Redeemer and to reveal the immeasurable riches of his glorious grace.

Finally, God freely and mercifully made this exchange. The catechism is careful to point out that the cause of God punishing Jesus in order to rescue us was "mere mercy." The language "mere mercy" means grace alone, grace apart from any other considerations. As the great preacher C. H. Spurgeon famously wrote, salvation is "all of grace." Although this grace trains us to avoid ungodliness, it does not depend upon our obedience in any way. As we consider the besetting sins and ongoing weaknesses of our lives, we have to cling to the "mere grace" aspect of the gospel. God did not give his beloved Son in view of what he would get out of our lives, but merely because he loves us. Now that's good news indeed!

Prayer

O Reconciling One, thank you for making a way for us. You have been perfect, both in justice and in mercy. We accept the salvation we do not deserve. We come before you in the name of Jesus Christ, your beloved Son, trusting in his merits rather than our own. Amen.

Question 20

Who is the Redeemer?

The only Redeemer is the Lord Jesus Christ, the eternal Son of God, in whom God became man and bore the penalty for sin himself.

📖 1 TIMOTHY 2:5

For there is one God, and there is one mediator between God and men, the man Christ Jesus.

💬 Commentary

JOHN CHRYSOSTOM

The Only Begotten, Who is before all ages, Who cannot be touched or be perceived, Who is simple, without body, has now put on my body, that is visible and liable to corruption. For what reason? That coming amongst us he may teach us, and teaching, lead us by the hand to the things that men cannot see. For since men believe that the eyes are more trustworthy than the ears, they doubt of that which they do not see, and so He has deigned to show Himself in bodily presence, that He may remove all doubt. . . . The Ancient of days has become an infant. He Who sits upon the sublime and heavenly Throne, now lies in a manger. And He Who cannot be touched, Who is simple, without complexity, and incorporeal, now lies subject to the hands of men. He Who has broken the bonds of sinners, is now bound by an infant's bands. But He has decreed that ignominy shall become honor, infamy be clothed with glory, and total humiliation the measure of His Goodness.

For this He assumed my body, that I may become capable of His Word; taking my flesh, He gives me His spirit; and so He bestowing and I receiving, He prepares for me the treasure of Life. He takes my flesh, to sanctify me; He gives me His Spirit, that He may save me.[25]

MARK DEVER

The Redeemer is Jesus Christ, the eternal Son of God. The eternal Son of God became man and lived a real human life like ours. For a little more than thirty years in the first century AD, he lived like you and me; the only difference is that he always trusted God. He trusted him entirely. So if you think of ways just yesterday and the day before that you should have trusted God and didn't, in those very times Jesus obeyed God. He trusted that what God knew was better, that he should follow his Father's will.

When I look back on my own life, I know that I haven't lived like that. But the Redeemer, Jesus Christ, has. He is called the Redeemer because he "re-deems" his people. He resets our value.

When you redeem something at a store, you turn it in and you get some money for it. When I was a kid, we had redemption stamps. We would save up our stamps and then turn them in to get something else. Well, Jesus is what sets our value. He resets our value. He gives his own life on the cross for all who repent of their sins and trust in him. He is our Redeemer. He has valued us, though we have thrown our own lives away by not trusting in our heavenly Father, by not obeying him, and by not fearing him. He actually came and gave his own life in our place. He lived a life of trust, and he died a death that he didn't have to die, but he did it because of his love for us. He gave himself entirely for us so he could, as the Bible says, be our Redeemer, the One who rescues us.

The image of redemption in the Old Testament is one of God rescuing his people from Egypt, pulling them out of bondage, out of literal slavery. In the New Testament Jesus the Redeemer rescues us from our natural state of being in bondage to sin, of serving ourselves in destructive ways. But God in his great love sent his only begotten Son, who lived a perfect life, died on the cross, and then rose from the dead in order to bring us to him, to redeem us. That's what we mean when we say Jesus Christ is our Redeemer.

Prayer

Precious Redeemer, before the world began, you loved us. You gave up your glory to bear our shame. You glorified your Father by obeying him all the way to the cross. You deserve our praise, thanks, and worship. We have no hope but in you. Amen.

Part 2

Christ, Redemption, Grace

Question 21

What sort of Redeemer
is needed to bring
us back to God?

One who is truly human and also truly God.

📖 ISAIAH 9:6

> For to us a child is born,
>   to us a son is given;
> and the government shall be upon his shoulder,
>   and his name shall be called
> Wonderful Counselor, Mighty God,
>   Everlasting Father, Prince of Peace.

💬 Commentary

AUGUSTINE OF HIPPO

He who existed as the Son of God before all ages, without a beginning, deigned to become the Son of Man in these recent years. He did this although He who submitted to such great evils for our sake had done no evil and although we, who were the recipients of so much good at His hands, had done nothing to merit these benefits. Begotten by the Father, He was not made by the Father; He was made Man in the Mother whom He Himself had made, so that He might exist here for a while, sprung from her who could never and nowhere have existed except through His power.[26]

BRYAN CHAPELL

Why do we need a Redeemer who is truly human? One reason is so that he can identify with us. The Bible says he was "in every respect . . . tempted as we are, yet without sin" (Heb. 4:15). He went through our experience, so he understands what we go through. He is our High Priest. He understands how we suffer. We understand that God can identify with us, but even as he identified with us—by having lived a hard life, by having been humiliated, and by having gone through humble circumstances—he did it with perfect obedience, not doubting the love of his Father and not wavering from his Father's path.

That means that not only could Jesus identify with what we experience as humans; he could become the perfect substitute for us. In my sin, I'm separated from God. He's holy; I am not. For God to be just and holy, he cannot identify with my sin. God had to provide a way for my sin to be put on another. He did that by having his Son come in human likeness, human form, but living perfectly so that he could be the substitute for my sin.

Because Jesus lived a perfect life, when he willingly suffered the penalty for my sin on the cross, it was a right, adequate, and perfect substitute for my sin and for your sin. Jesus could identify with what we go through, but because he lived perfectly in obedience, he became the perfect substitute for our sin. And because he took our sin upon himself, having identified with us, when he rose from the grave and ascended to his Father, he became the perfect advocate for us. He knows our strengths and our weaknesses. Because he retains his humanlike features and functions in his divine nature, he still understands the entirety of our human experience and knows exactly what we need.

But he's also God. And because Jesus is God, he can accomplish the purposes for which he came. Even now, he can rule our world in such a way that all God intends for our lives will happen. And when he was put to death because he was God, he could not only fully pay the sacrifice for our sin and pay the debt that we owed, he could rise from the grave. Death could not defeat him. Because Jesus is alive, because he is sovereign, because he is divine and risen to God, he continues to advocate for us. But even more than advocate, Jesus accomplishes God's purposes in our lives. He is the God who *accomplishes* all that we need, even as he is the man who *understands* all that we need and *provides* all that we need.

Jesus, perfect God, perfect man, is the Redeemer that we needed, and he accomplished all that was necessary by identifying with our humanity and doing what God had to do to save us.

✋ Prayer

Son of God and Son of Man, for generations you were prophesied. Only One who is both divine and human could live in perfect obedience and be a fitting sacrifice on our behalf. There is no other way to God but by you. Amen.

Question 22

Why must the Redeemer be truly human?

That in human nature he might on our behalf perfectly obey the whole law and suffer the punishment for human sin; and also that he might sympathize with our weaknesses.

📖 HEBREWS 2:17

Therefore he had to be made like his brothers in every respect, so that he might become a merciful and faithful high priest in the service of God, to make propitiation for the sins of the people.

💬 Commentary

ATHANASIUS OF ALEXANDRIA

For the Word, perceiving that no otherwise could the corruption of men be undone save by death as a necessary condition, while it was impossible for the Word to suffer death, being immortal, and Son of the Father; to this end He takes to Himself a body capable of death, that it, by partaking of the Word Who is above all, might be worthy to die in the stead of all, and might, because of the Word which was come to dwell in it, remain incorruptible, and that thenceforth corruption might be stayed from all by the Grace of the Resurrection. Whence, by offering unto death the body He Himself had taken, as an offering and sacrifice free from any stain, straightway He put away death from all His peers by the offering of an equivalent. For being over all, the Word of God naturally by offering His own temple and corporeal instrument for the life of all satisfied the debt by His death. And thus He, the incorruptible Son of God, being conjoined with all by a like nature, naturally clothed all with incorruption, by the promise of the resurrection.[27]

THABITI ANYABWILE

We human people are so fallen, and we've been so fallen for so long, that we actually think that we are the measure of what it means to be human. It's striking. We say things like "to err is human." And we unwittingly then begin to define humanity in terms of that fallenness, in terms of its brokenness, in terms of its incompleteness. But if you define humanity like that, what do you do with Jesus? What do you do with Jesus who takes upon himself our humanity, yet, as the Bible tells us, is without sin, who does not err?

What we see in Jesus is true humanity. What we see in his incarnation, his earthly life and ministry, is what humanity was meant to be, what Adam was created to be but ruined in his sin and his fall. So, as Romans 5 teaches, the first man Adam sins, and through his sin death enters the world. But here comes a second Adam, a true Adam, Christ, who is truly man. What Christ does in his humanity is nothing short of remarkable. In his humanity, he offers to God everything that we owe God. In his humanity, in his perfect obedience to God's commands, he offers to God the obedience that we refuse to give him (and could not give him) because of our fallen, sinful nature.

It's absolutely essential that what we see in Christ is perfect righteousness, because he's supplying that righteousness on our behalf. All the righteousness we will ever need is in the Son of God who took upon himself our flesh, our likeness, our human nature. Not only does he positively supply the righteousness, but on the cross, our Savior dies and pays the penalty that humanity owed. He dies in our place. We owe God not only righteousness, but now because we didn't supply that righteousness, we also owe God our lives, our death, our blood. Christ takes our place, and he supplies to God the sacrifice on our behalf that satisfies God's demands for righteousness and his righteous determination to punish sin.

And so in order to be for us a perfect High Priest, in order to be for us a perfect offering, Jesus had to be one with us. He had to take upon himself our nature and in that nature demonstrate what humanity is, what it was meant to be—righteous before God, obedient to God, worshiping God in all things, loving him fully. And he also demonstrates what humanity owes when he pays the penalty on Calvary's cross for our sin. And so to be that High Priest, a perfect High Priest, who also now sympathizes with us, knows our suffering, knows our failures, knows our troubles, and knows them intimately because he experienced them in our flesh, he can look to humanity with sympathy and represent humanity to God with perfection.

And so it was necessary that he be made like us in every way, but without sin.

🤲 Prayer

Faithful High Priest, you were tempted in every way as we are, yet you remained perfect in your obedience. Thank you that you know our weakness. Keep us from excusing or denying our sinfulness. We joyfully accept your exchange. Amen.

Question 23

Why must the Redeemer be truly God?

That because of his divine nature his obedience and suffering would be perfect and effective; and also that he would be able to bear the righteous anger of God against sin and yet overcome death.

📖 ACTS 2:24

God raised him up, loosing the pangs of death, because it was not possible for him to be held by it.

💬 Commentary

JOHN CHRYSOSTOM

Let no one weep for his iniquities, for pardon hath shone forth from the grave. Let no one fear death, for the Saviour's death hath set us free. In as much as he was held captive of it, he hath annihilated it. By descending into Hell, He made Hell captive. He angered it when it tasted of his flesh. And Isaiah, foretelling this, did cry: Hell, said he, was angered, when it encountered thee. . . . It was angered, for it was abolished. It was angered, for it was mocked. It was angered, for it

Christ, Redemption, Grace

was slain. It was angered, for it was fettered in chains. It took a body, and met God face to face. It took earth, and encountered Heaven. It took that which was visible, and fell upon the invisible. O Death, where is thy sting? O Hell, where is thy victory? Christ is risen, and thou art overthrown. Christ is risen, and the demons are fallen. Christ is risen, and the Angels rejoice. Christ is risen, and life reigneth.[28]

LEO SCHUSTER

We often like to focus on the human aspects of Jesus, and it's important to remember that Jesus was fully human. But he was also fully God. What does it mean that Jesus was fully God? And why is it so important that he, as our Redeemer, be truly God?

The apostle John opens his Gospel by declaring that Jesus is the eternal God in flesh. He explains: "In the beginning was the Word, and the Word was with God, and the Word was God. . . . The Word became flesh and dwelt among us, and we have seen his glory, glory as of the only Son from the Father, full of grace and truth" (1:1, 14). In his letter to the Colossians the apostle Paul wrote, "For in him the whole fullness of deity dwells bodily" (Col. 2:9).

Similarly, Jesus himself numerous times affirmed his divinity and that he was one with the Father. On one occasion, some of his listeners understood what he was claiming and tried to stone him, explaining that they were stoning him not for any good work, but for blasphemy:, "You, being a man, make yourself God" (John 10:33). The book of Revelation describes Jesus as the Alpha and the Omega, the One "who was and is and is to come" (1:8). Indeed, he is no mere man. He is truly God.

So why is it so important that Jesus as our Redeemer be truly God? Our sin was committed against God. Only God can forgive a transgression against himself. This is why some of the religious leaders in Jesus's day were horrified when he said he forgave sins. They understood the implications of what he said. How could a mere man forgive the sin we have against God? A mere man can't, but God can.

Jesus needed to be fully human in order to be our substitute, but he needed to be fully God in order for his obedience and suffering to be perfect and for God's justice to be completely and eternally satisfied.

🤲 Prayer

God the Son, because of our sin, we could never bear the wrath of God or overcome death. Only you, the Holy One, could suffer the just punishment for sin and defeat death. Thank you for making a way for us to God, to enjoy him eternally. Amen.

Question 24

Why was it necessary for Christ, the Redeemer, to die?

Since death is the punishment for sin, Christ died willingly in our place to deliver us from the power and penalty of sin and bring us back to God. By his substitutionary atoning death, he alone redeems us from hell and gains for us forgiveness of sin, righteousness, and everlasting life.

📖 COLOSSIANS 1:21–22

And you, who once were alienated and hostile in mind, doing evil deeds, he has now reconciled in his body of flesh by his death, in order to present you holy and blameless and above reproach before him.

💬 Commentary

ATHANASIUS OF ALEXANDRIA

Thus, taking a body like our own, because all our bodies were liable to the corruption of death, He surrendered His body to death instead of all, and offered it to the Father. This He did out of sheer love for us, so that in His death all might die, and the law of death thereby be abolished because, having fulfilled in His body that for which it was appointed, it was thereafter voided of its power for men. This He did that He might turn again to incorruption men who had turned back to corruption, and make them alive through death by the appropriation of His body and by the grace of His resurrection. Thus He would make death to disappear from them as utterly as straw from fire.[29]

MARK DEVER

Why was it necessary for Christ, the Redeemer, to die? This is a heavy question. I don't know if questions get much heavier than this. Christ lived a perfect life, the life you and I should have lived. He lived a life of love, of service. He lived an amazing life of trust in his heavenly Father. So the question is a pressing one. Why should one like that die? Why was it morally necessary?

Well, he didn't have to die for his own sake. If we were thinking just about Jesus, there would be no necessity for the cross. No, he died because he would be the Redeemer. It was his will, and also his heavenly Father's will, to redeem us. It was his will to lay down his life, to sacrifice himself by dying on the cross in order to rescue us from the penalty that we deserved. You see, because God is good, he will punish sin. That wrong thing that you or I have done in secret—God knows about it. God's real. He's not just an idea. He's not just a figment of our imagination. And this God is so thoroughly committed to what is good and right that every sin will be punished. And this is where Jesus comes in. Jesus determined to be our Redeemer. It was the will of his heavenly Father that he give himself as a sacrifice in substitution. That's a word that's often used—as a substitute, in the place of, instead of you and me. Jesus is our substitute if we repent of our sins, turn from them and trust in him.

So why did the Redeemer need to die? Because that's the only way you and I would live.

🖐 Prayer

Atoning Savior, thank you that you didn't turn back, but endured all the way to death on the cross, and beyond. Because of your death, we can live eternally. With this knowledge, help us face our own deaths with courage, faith, and hope. Amen.

Question 25

Does Christ's death
mean all our sins
can be forgiven?

Yes, because Christ's death on the cross fully paid the penalty for
our sin, God graciously imputes Christ's righteousness to us as if it
were our own and will remember our sins no more.

📖 **2 CORINTHIANS 5:21**

For our sake he made him to be sin who knew no sin, so that in him
we might become the righteousness of God.

🗨 **Commentary**

RICHARD SIBBES

Though one sin was enough to bring condemnation, yet the free
gift of grace in Christ is of many offences unto justification. And
we have a sure ground for this, for the righteousness of Christ is
God's righteousness, and God will thus glorify it, that it shall stand
good to those that by faith apply it against their daily sins, even

till at once we cease both to live and sin. For this very end was the Son of God willingly made sin, that we might be freed from the same. And if all our sins laid upon Christ could not take away God's love from him, shall they take away God's love from us, when by Christ's blood our souls are purged from them? O mercy of all mercies, that . . . he would vouchsafe to . . . make us his by such a way, as all the angels in heaven stand wondering at; even his Son not only taking our nature and miserable condition, but our sin upon him, that that being done away, we might through Christ have boldness with God as ours, who is now in heaven appearing there for us, until he bring us home to himself, and presents us to his Father for *his* for ever![30]

ALISTAIR BEGG

Some years ago when I was diagnosed with cancer, my great concern was that the surgeon would get it all. I wasn't really interested in a cure that was only partial. And when we think about Jesus bearing our sins, the mystery and the wonder of the gospel is that he deals with all of them. He who was absolutely perfect died in the place of sinners, identifying with us in our guilt and becoming liable to our punishment. When Paul writes to the Corinthians, he tells them that God was not counting their sins against them. And the reason for that is because he was counting them against *him*. Jesus died not as a martyr, but as a substitute. The invitation of the gospel is given to all, but the assurance of forgiveness is only for those who are in Christ, whose sins have been counted to him.

Augustus Toplady captured the security of this when he wrote:

Rock of ages cleft for me,
let me hide myself in Thee;
let the water and the blood,
from thy riven side which flowed,
be of sin the double cure;
cleanse me from its guilt and power.[31]

114

Peter tells us that the angels, actually, long to look into this (1 Pet. 1:12). And what they have observed from a distance, the believer knows perfectly.

The wonder of it all is that our disobedience is completely covered by the obedience of the Lord Jesus—all of our sins dealt with forever.

Prayer

Forgiving Father, when we are covered in the righteousness of Christ, you remember our sins no more. You have put them as far as the east is from the west. Help us not to doubt your forgiveness, your mercy, or your love, but come to you boldly as your beloved children. Amen.

Question 26

What else does Christ's death redeem?

Christ's death is the beginning of the redemption and renewal of every part of fallen creation, as he powerfully directs all things for his own glory and creation's good.

📖 COLOSSIANS 1:19–20

For in him all the fullness of God was pleased to dwell, and through him to reconcile to himself all things, whether on earth or in heaven, making peace by the blood of his cross.

💬 Commentary

JOHN BUNYAN

Jesus is a Redeemer, that is his name; he came into the world on this very business, to redeem his people, to redeem them from all iniquity (Titus 2:14), from this present evil world, from our vain conversations. He hath shed his precious blood to purchase us, we are bought with a price (1 Cor. 6:20). We are none of our own, we are his, the purchase of his blood; and we may be confident that he dearly loves us, for he dearly bought us; and if he had not dearly loved us, he would never have given himself for us (Gal. 2:20). That was the highest testimony of his love; he loved us, and washed us from our sins in his blood (Rev. 1:5). He will redeem us from the wrath to come.[32]

VERMON PIERRE

Many pictures have been taken of the Grand Canyon. But none of them can really do it justice. The Grand Canyon is just one of those things best experienced in person. You can see it on people's faces as they walk up to the rim and look out over the Canyon for the first time. They can't help but be immediately struck by its immensity and unique beauty. It is a truly awe-inspiring sight.

Yet even there, standing at the rim, looking out over the Canyon, you won't get a full experience of the place. It's when you actually go down into the Canyon that you begin to see that it is bigger and deeper, more glorious in fact, than you initially saw. The view of the Grand Canyon at the rim is just the beginning of the even grander view that you will experience once you travel into the Canyon.

So it is with the gospel. As we first step up to the gospel, we see a most beautiful and awe-inspiring sight—the salvation of sinners. More specifically, that God through Jesus Christ has graciously acted to save a sinful people unto himself. These people are redeemed from sin and made a new creation and are adopted forever into the family of God.

It's an amazing, beautiful, incredible message. And, at the same time, it is just the beginning of God's saving, redeeming, and renewing work. As we head deeper into the gospel, a fuller and even more glorious picture emerges. We see that God's saving of sinners was always intended to open up into a deeper, wider, all-encompassing saving of the whole creation.

The saving of sinners is at the heart of the gospel. It is the fountainhead. And from this fountainhead flows a mighty river, one full of redemptive, healing power for every square inch of the cosmos.

How is this possible? Through "his blood, shed on the cross" (Col. 1:20). Creation was in bondage due to the fall of man, locked behind the gates of hell. But then God moves toward us and, using the cross of Jesus Christ, smashes down those gates! Through God's gracious efforts, a people and indeed a whole creation are freed. They are now in the kingdom of the Son, a place of complete redemption and total renewal.

All of this does two things for us.

1. It gives us hope about the future. All around us we see evidence of the fall in things like unjust social systems and moral cultural decline and terrible suffering and death. The gospel message in its fullest form tells us not to despair but to have a sure and certain hope that one day all such things will be wiped away and replaced with peace and harmony, with the "healing of the nations" (Rev. 22:2).

This hope, however, is mixed with a warning. For the fallen creation includes many who are still opposed to God, who continue to reject his rule and the One he sent to rule, Jesus. The redeeming work of the gospel means that all things, including those who oppose the Lord, will eventually be brought to heel. The question every person faces now is whether that redeeming work will be experienced with joyful awe or with the painful gnashing of teeth.

2. It gives us motivation in the present. The creation has not been abandoned by God. Instead, through Jesus, it has been reclaimed by him and will eventually be made brand new. It will be a creation characterized by harmony and peace, rightly related to God and humanity. The church today is an early outpost of this new creation and a primary means toward bringing about this new creation.

This means then that the church is not a passive bystander to the world. Nor is it an imperiled passenger in the world, only biding its time until it is rescued off of the sinking creation. Instead, the church is a divinely commissioned community of people whose faithful efforts in the world even now matter, insofar as they proclaim and embody the redeeming and renewing power of the gospel.

🖐 Prayer

Creation's Redeemer, the world will not always be as it is now, fallen and groaning for the fullness of your kingdom. Thank you that, ultimately, you will make all things new. We rejoice that your redemption extends to the world you have made. Amen.

Question 27

Are all people, just as they were lost through Adam, saved through Christ?

No, only those who are elected by God and united to Christ by faith. Nevertheless God in his mercy demonstrates common grace even to those who are not elect, by restraining the effects of sin and enabling works of culture for human well-being.

📖 ROMANS 5:17

For if, because of one man's trespass, death reigned through that one man, much more will those who receive the abundance of grace and the free gift of righteousness reign in life through the one man Jesus Christ.

💬 Commentary

MARTYN LLOYD-JONES

Common grace is the term applied to those general blessings which God imparts to all men and women indiscriminately as He pleases, not only to His own people, but to all men and women, according

121

to His own will. Or, again, common grace means those general operations of the Holy Spirit in which, without renewing the heart, He exercises a moral influence whereby sin is restrained, order is maintained in social life, and civil righteousness is promoted. That is the general definition. The Holy Spirit has been operative in this world from the very beginning and He has had His influence and His effect upon men and women who are not saved and who have gone to perdition. While they were in this life and world they came under these general, non-saving operations of the Holy Spirit. . . . It is not a saving influence, nor is it a redemptive influence, but it is a part of God's purpose. . . . If the Holy Spirit were not operative in men and women in this general way, human beings, as a result of the Fall and of sin, would have festered away into oblivion long ago. . . . Next to that is what is generally described as culture. By that I mean arts and science, an interest in the things of the mind, literature, architecture, sculpture, painting, and music. Now, there can be no question at all but that cultivation of the arts is good. It is not redemptive, but it improves people, it makes them live better lives. Now, where do all these things come from? How do you explain men like Shakespeare or Michelangelo? The answer from the Scripture is that all these people had their gifts and were able to exercise them as the result of the operation of common grace, this general influence of the Holy Spirit.[33]

TIMOTHY KELLER

This particular catechism answer strikes a very helpful balance. On the one hand, we learn that not all human beings will be saved. This is taught so clearly in the Bible in so many places that it's impossible to list all the texts. But let me call your attention to two.

In John 6, Jesus says, "And this is the will of him who sent me, that I should lose nothing of all that he has given me, but raise it up on the last day" (v. 39). Jesus is talking about coming for a very specific number of people that he's been given, and he's going to raise them up on the last day. Not everyone will be raised up on the last day.

Romans 8:28–30 teaches a similar thing. Paul says in verse 30:

"Those whom he predestined he also called, and those whom he called he also justified, and those whom he justified he also glorified." Notice, it's the same number all through. He doesn't say some of those he called, he justified, as if there were this many called and this many justified. No. All—and only—those he called, he justified. All—and only—those he justified he glorified. It's a definite number. Not all people will be saved.

On the other hand, this catechism answer talks about common grace. Richard Mouw defines that in his book on this subject: "Is there a non-saving grace that is at work in the broader reaches of human cultural interaction, a grace that expedites a desire on God's part to bestow certain blessings on all human beings—elect and non-elect alike, blessings that provide the basis for Christians to cooperate with and learn from non-Christians?"[34]

And the Bible's answer, in places like Romans 1 and 2, is yes. Though not all people are going to be saved, God still gives his gifts of wisdom and insight across the face of the whole human race. Through art and through science and through good government and in other ways, God is making this world a far better place than it would be if only Christians had those gifts. And so, again, here's that very helpful balance that we should strike. On the one hand, no, not everyone is to be saved. No, not everyone has the saving grace of Jesus Christ in their lives. But on the other hand, we must appreciate the common grace that God gives across the whole human race. We must see that God is helping us and helping in the world through many people who do not believe. We need to appreciate those. We must be grateful for them, and we must respect them. That's the balance that we must strike.

Prayer

Sovereign Savior, there is salvation in no one but you, and you save everyone who calls upon your name. We would never have called upon you if you had not brought us from death to life. We do not fully understand your electing love, but we confess that neither we nor anyone else deserves it. Amen.

Question 28

What happens after death to those not united to Christ by faith?

At the day of judgment they will receive the fearful but just sentence of condemnation pronounced against them. They will be cast out from the favorable presence of God, into hell, to be justly and grievously punished, forever.

📖 JOHN 3:16–18, 36

For God so loved the world, that he gave his only Son, that whoever believes in him should not perish but have eternal life. For God did not send his Son into the world to condemn the world, but in order that the world might be saved through him. Whoever believes in him is not condemned, but whoever does not believe is condemned already, because he has not believed in the name of the only Son of God. . . . Whoever believes in the Son has eternal life; whoever does not obey the Son shall not see life, but the wrath of God remains on him.

💬 Commentary

J. C. RYLE

Painful as the subject of hell is, it is one about which I dare not, cannot, must not be silent. Who would desire to speak of hell-fire if God had not spoken of it? When God has spoken of it so plainly, who can safely hold his peace?

. . . I know that some do not believe there is any hell at all. They think it impossible there can be such a place. They call it inconsistent with the mercy of God. They say it is too awful an idea to be really true. The devil of course rejoices in the views of such people. They help his kingdom mightily. They are preaching up his old favourite doctrine, "ye shall not surely die." . . .

There is but one point to be settled, "what says the word of God." Do you believe the Bible? Then depend upon it, *hell is real and true.* It is as true as heaven—as true as justification by faith—as true as the fact that Christ died upon the cross—as true as the Dead Sea. There is not a fact or doctrine which you may not lawfully doubt if you doubt hell. Disbelieve hell, and you unscrew, unsettle, and unpin everything in Scripture. You may as well throw your Bible aside at once. From "no hell" to "no God" there is but a series of steps.[35]

JOHN LIN

One of the Bible's more difficult and often misunderstood teachings is that of hell being a real, conscious, eternal punishment. And this is understandable. All of us have people in our midst who don't know Christ—friends, family members, neighbors, colleagues—about whom we would rather not think that hell could be their future. In fact, people have had discomfort about the idea of hell throughout history, because on the surface it seems inconsistent with everything we read in the Bible about God's mercy and love. And yet the Bible's teaching on hell as conscious and eternal suffering is unavoidable. Actually, without the existence of hell, much of what we know about God's love comes into question.

First, Jesus, the most loving man who ever lived, spoke about hell more frequently and vividly than all other biblical authors combined. He described it as Gehenna, which was a garbage heap where fires burned constantly, or as the outer darkness, where there's no illumination but only misery. In the story he tells of the rich man and Lazarus, hell is a place of conscious and real suffering. Jesus warns us about hell again and again (Matt. 13:41–42; Mark 9:42–48; Luke 16:19–31).

Second, the existence of hell helps us to understand the consequences of sin. In some ways hell is the outworking of what we as sinful people have always wanted: autonomy and independence from God. In hell we are therefore cut off from God and from everything that God is. So in hell there's no love, there's no friendship, there's no joy, there's no rest, because those are all things that exist only where God is present.

But most importantly, until we acknowledge the reality of hell, we cannot truly understand the meaning of the cross. Put another way, we cannot understand God's love until we understand the reality of his wrath. God's wrath is a settled, controlled opposition and hatred of anything that is destroying what he loves. God's wrath flows from his love for creation. It flows from his justice. He's angry at greed, self-centeredness, injustice, and evil because they're destructive. And God will not tolerate anything or anyone responsible for destroying the creation and the people that he loves.

Think of it this way. Saying, "I know God loves me because he would give up everything for me" is much different from saying, "I know God loves me because he *did* give up everything for me." One is a loving sentiment; the other is a loving act. And while we may try to make God more loving by diminishing the reality of hell and God's wrath, all we've really done is diminish the love of God. Without a real hell we can't understand the real price that Jesus paid for our sin. And without a real price that was paid, there's no real love, there's no real grace, and there's no real praise for what he has done.

Unless you believe in hell, you'll never know how much Jesus loves you and how much he values you. Jesus experienced hell himself on the cross. Jesus was separated from his Father. On the cross Jesus cried, "My God, My God, why have you forsaken me?" (Matt. 27:46). When Jesus lost the eternal love of the Father, he experienced an agony, a disintegration, an isolation greater than anything anyone of us would have experienced in eternity in hell. He took the isolation and disintegration that we deserve upon himself. Unless you believe in hell and see what Jesus took for you, you will never know how much he loves you.

The real issue is not how a loving God would allow there to be a hell. The issue is, if Jesus Christ would experience hell for me, then, truly, he must be a loving God. It's not "Why would God allow hell?" It's "Why would God experience hell for me?" And yet he did.

Prayer

Judge of All the Earth, we tremble to think of the judgment that awaits all outside your covenant. Before it is too late, may those we love be reconciled to you so that they do not suffer the punishment that is theirs, and would have been ours, apart from you. Amen.

Question 29

How can we be saved?

Only by faith in Jesus Christ and in his substitutionary atoning death on the cross; so even though we are guilty of having disobeyed God and are still inclined to all evil, nevertheless, God, without any merit of our own but only by pure grace, imputes to us the perfect righteousness of Christ when we repent and believe in him.

📖 EPHESIANS 2:8–9

For by grace you have been saved through faith. And this is not your own doing; it is the gift of God, not a result of works, so that no one may boast.

💬 Commentary

CHARLES HADDON SPURGEON

Being justified by faith, we have peace with God. Conscience accuses no longer. Judgment now decides for the sinner instead of against him. Memory looks back upon past sins, with deep sorrow for the sin, but yet with no dread of any penalty to come; for Christ has paid the debt of his people to the last jot and tittle, and received the divine receipt; and unless God can be so unjust as to demand double payment for one debt, no soul for whom Jesus died as a substitute can ever be cast into hell. It seems to be one of the very principles of our enlightened nature to believe that God is just; we feel that it must be so, and this gives us our terror at first; but is it not marvelous that this very same belief that God is just, becomes afterwards the pillar of our confidence and peace! If God is just, I, a sinner, alone and without a substitute, must be punished; but Jesus stands in my place and is punished for me; and now, if God is just, I, a sinner, standing in Christ, can never be punished. God must change his nature before one soul for whom Jesus was a substitute can ever by any possibility suffer the lash of the law. Therefore, Jesus having taken the place of the believer—having rendered a full equivalent to divine wrath for all that his people ought to have suffered as the result of sin, the believer can shout with glorious triumph, "Who shall lay anything to the charge of God's elect?" Not God, for he has justified; not Christ, for he has died, "yes rather has risen again." My hope does not live because I am not a sinner, but because I am a sinner for whom Christ died; my trust is not that I am holy, but that being unholy, he is my righteousness. My faith does not rest upon what I am, or shall be, or feel, or know, but in what Christ is, in what he has done, and in what he is now doing for me. On the lion of justice the fair maid of hope rides like a queen.[36]

KEVIN DEYOUNG

In Acts 16, Paul and Silas are in prison when a violent earthquake occurs. Prisoners are escaping, and the jailer wakes up and is absolutely dismayed that everyone is running off. The jailer is about to kill himself, and Paul stops him. And the jailer asks this very famous question: "Sirs, what must I do to be saved?" (v. 30). Paul gives him the short, biblical, absolutely beautiful answer: "Believe in the Lord Jesus and you will be saved, you and your household" (v. 31).

"What must I do to be saved?" There's no more important question in this life or for the next life. The answer to our catechism question provides a wonderful summary of what it means to have faith in Christ—the sort of faith that saves—and how God saves through faith. This summary contains two key words. First is the very first word: *only*. Only faith in Jesus Christ. You see, it wouldn't be terribly controversial to talk about faith. People are into faith and believing something. But it's *only* faith, not faith plus something else. It's not faith in addition to your background, faith plus your family of origin, faith plus how many good things you can do for social justice, or faith plus how often you pray. It's only faith, and it's faith in Jesus Christ—there is an object to it.

Many people will wax on and on about faith and belief and say, "I'm a person of faith" or "You've got to have faith." But faith by itself doesn't mean anything. It is the object of faith that saves us. It's not being a person who has strong beliefs, who is sincere, or who has a mystical belief in spiritual things that saves us. It's faith in Jesus Christ. He's the object. It's the object of our faith that saves us. Faith is only an instrument. It's not the one good deed that God sees and says, "Well, you don't have much going for you, but you have faith, and I really like that." No. Faith is what joins us to Christ, and then he saves us. It's the object that matters.

Growing up in a cold part of the country, I often went ice skating and played hockey. I might tiptoe out onto that first freeze of the year, and sort of wonder, "Is this ice thick enough?" Someone else might be on the ice zipping around skating with great freedom and having a lot of faith in the ice, while I'm gingerly tiptoeing and have just enough faith to get out on the ice. But what makes both of us secure? It's not the level of faith, though you'd like to have the strong faith that's zipping around there, but it's the thickness of the ice.

It's the object on which you're standing that saves you. And that's Jesus Christ. So it's only faith in him.

The other word that is so crucial here is *imputes*. It is essential to the gospel and to the Christian faith that the righteous life that Christ lived is imputed to us. That means it's reckoned to us. It's counted to us. It's sort of a wire transfer of funds. And there's a difference between a righteousness that is inherent in us, infused in us, a kind of righteousness that says, "Well, look at me, I'm righteous. I do righteous things." That's not what this is talking about. This is talking about the righteousness of Christ that is outside of us, but because we're joined to Jesus by faith, it gets counted as our righteousness, so that God can be both the just and the justifier of the wicked.

That's the problem in Romans 3, and that's the good news of the gospel—that though we are still sinners, God justifies us. And he is just to do so not because he waves a magic wand or says sin's not a big deal (wink-wink); it's because we belong to Christ and his righteousness is our righteousness that God can be just and we can be justified.

Prayer

Merciful One, we renounce our pride and all pretensions of self-righteousness, and we come to you in repentance and faith. We trust your death to give us life. We praise you for the gift of salvation. Amen.

Question 30

What is faith in Jesus Christ?

Faith in Jesus Christ is acknowledging the truth of everything that God has revealed in his Word, trusting in him, and also receiving and resting on him alone for salvation as he is offered to us in the gospel.

📖 GALATIANS 2:20

I have been crucified with Christ. It is no longer I who live, but Christ who lives in me. And the life I now live in the flesh I live by faith in the Son of God, who loved me and gave himself for me.

🗨 Commentary

JONATHAN EDWARDS

Upon the whole, the best, and clearest, and most perfect definition of justifying faith, and most according to the Scripture, that I can think of, is this, faith is the soul's entirely embracing the revelation of Jesus Christ as our Saviour. The word embrace is a metaphorical expression; but I think it is much clearer than any proper expression whatsoever; it is called believing, because believing is the first act of the soul in embracing a narration or revelation: and embracing, when conversant about a revelation or thing declared, is more properly called believing, than loving or choosing. If it were conversant about a person only, it would be more properly called loving. If it were conversant about a gift, an inheritance, or reward, it would more properly be called receiving or accepting.

The definition might have been expressed in these words: faith is the soul's entirely adhering and acquiescing in the revelation of Jesus Christ as our Saviour—Or thus: faith is the soul's embracing that truth of God, that reveals Jesus Christ as our Saviour—Or thus: faith is the soul's entirely acquiescing in, and depending upon, the truth of God, revealing Christ as our Saviour.

It is the whole soul according and assenting to the truth, and embracing of it. There is an entire yielding of the mind and heart to the revelation, and a closing with it, and adhering to it, with the belief, and with the inclination and affection.[37]

JOHN YATES

Sometimes I wonder if we realize what a really big word *salvation* is. What does it mean to be saved? What's the meaning of salvation?

It means *safe*. But it also mean *healed*. It means *forgiven*. It means *adopted*. It means *having been made whole*. It's a big word. It means that we are *restored in our relationship with God*. We've been given life with God now, and we've also been given the gift of eternal life with God in heaven forever. So salvation is big. Salvation is a gift of God. It's not something that we can earn, even though that's the way many people feel about it. It is not something we can achieve, but something that has to be received. And we need to have that straight from the very beginning.

Salvation can come instantaneously, as it did for Zacchaeus when Jesus entered into his house. Jesus said, "Today salvation has come to this house" (Luke 19:9). It can come in a moment of realization and faith. But it is something that is lived out over the course of a lifetime. There's a story about an old English bishop who was walking down a London street when a sidewalk evangelist said to him, "Sir, have you been saved?" The old man's answer is significant. According to the story, he stopped and thought and then in a very gracious way said, "Yes, I have been saved. I am being saved, and I shall be saved." What did he mean? He meant he could look back on a moment in time when he put faith in Christ and turned to him in faith and hope, and he experienced salvation. But he also meant that salvation was something he was living and experiencing more of every day. And salvation was something he was going to enter into more fully when he went to be with the Lord in the next life.

Salvation begins when God opens our eyes to begin to grasp how much we need Christ. As long as we think we can save ourselves, the way is closed off. Being saved is like being in the midst of drowning and realizing you can't save yourself and someone has to come along and rescue you, and you just have to relax and be rescued because you're over your head and you can't swim and you're going to drown otherwise. The only thing I can contribute to my salvation is my own sinful nature. It's about coming to God with an awareness of our humble need—coming in faith, repenting of my sins, and laying out before God my sense that I need him. That's the beginning of salvation.

Paul says in Romans 10 that everyone who calls upon the name of the Lord will be saved. We live in a time when many people reject the idea that faith in Christ is necessary in order to become a child of God and an inheritor of eternal life. And yet Jesus said, "I am the way and the truth and the life. No one comes to the Father but by me." He is our pathway to salvation.

This was the message of the apostles. As Peter preached in Acts 4: "There is no other name by which we may be saved." Salvation comes through Jesus Christ.

✋ Prayer

Author of Our Faith, we believe that you are who you say you are. Your Word is truth, and it reveals you as our only hope of salvation. We believe your promises, walking by faith, not by sight. Amen.

What do we believe by true faith?

Everything taught to us in the gospel. The Apostles' Creed expresses what we believe in these words: We believe in God the Father Almighty, Maker of heaven and earth; and in Jesus Christ his only Son our Lord, who was conceived by the Holy Spirit, born of the virgin Mary, suffered under Pontius Pilate, was crucified, died, and was buried. He descended into hell. The third day he rose again from the dead. He ascended into heaven, and is seated at the right hand of God the Father Almighty; from there he will come to judge the living and the dead. We believe in the Holy Spirit, the holy catholic church, the communion of saints, the forgiveness of sins, the resurrection of the body, and the life everlasting.

📖 JUDE 3

I found it necessary to write appealing to you to contend for the faith that was once for all delivered to the saints.

⬛ Commentary

JOHN WESLEY

But what is faith? Not an opinion, no more than it is a form of words; not any number of opinions put together, be they ever so true. A string of opinions is no more Christian faith, than a string of beads is Christian holiness. It is not an assent to any opinion, or any number of opinions. A man may assent to three, or three-and-twenty creeds: he may assent to all the Old and New Testament (at least, as far as he understands them) and yet have no Christian faith at all.

. . . Christian faith . . . is a divine evidence or conviction wrought in the heart, that God is reconciled to me through his Son; inseparably joined with a confidence in him, as a gracious reconciled Father, as for all things, so especially for all those good things which are invisible and eternal. To believe (in the Christian sense) is, then, to walk in the light of eternity; and to have a clear sight of, and confidence in, the Most High, reconciled to me through the Son of his love.[38]

D. A. CARSON

"We believe in God the Father Almighty, Maker of heaven and earth." So begins what is universally called the Apostles' Creed. Strictly speaking, it was not formulated by the apostles. It emerged in the second century. But it is called the Apostles' Creed because the summary of what is given in the creed reflects the doctrine of the apostles, the doctrine of the New Testament in summary form. It's an early Christian confession. But it is so early, and has been used so widely across Christian denominations all around the world, that it is one of the rare things that unites all Christians in common belief.

If you read it through carefully and slowly, you'll see there's explicit mention of the Father and of the Son and of the Holy Spirit, of creation, the virgin birth, the coming of Christ, his rising from the dead, who Christians are, what it means to have the Holy Spirit working within us, and so forth, all in very brief compass in words that millions and millions of Christians have either memorized or recite every Sunday or sometimes use as part of their private devotions.

It's important to remember that creeds are shaped, at least in part, by the era in which they are formulated, not because the Bible changes, but because the questions that we ask of the Bible change just a wee bit from time to time. Other creedal statements, for example, that were made at the time of the Reformation in the sixteenth century ask and answer slightly different questions. But the Apostles' Creed is regularly said by Christians all around the world because it was written so early that it was used before a lot of the later important doctrinal divisions set in. And within this framework, it very ably summarizes the gospel in just a few sentences. In some ways it is a kind of second-century attempt to recapitulate what we read, for example, in the opening verses of 1 Corinthians 15, which itself is a very simple creed. What is the gospel? Paul asks. Well, first, Christ died for our sins according to the Scriptures, and then various things are added and added and added until we have a summary of the great good news and its content—that God in the fullness of time sent forth his Son to die on the cross, rise from the dead, and bring to himself a vast number of the people that Paul calls the new humanity.

So when you gather for public worship on the Lord's Day and recite the creed, remember that behind the mere words on the page are two thousand years of Christian history. The creed serves to link Christians across cultures and languages and space and time as together we say we believe in God the Father Almighty, Maker of heaven and earth.

Prayer

Maker of Heaven and Earth, make the startling claims of our faith come alive to us. Let us not divorce theological truth from the history of your salvation, which occurred in time and space. Let us not waiver in unbelief, but rest our lives upon the truth that you raise the dead. Amen.

Question 32

What do justification and sanctification mean?

Justification means our declared righteousness before God, made possible by Christ's death and resurrection for us. Sanctification means our gradual, growing righteousness, made possible by the Spirit's work in us.

📖 1 PETER 1:1–2

To those who are elect exiles . . . according to the foreknowledge of God the Father, in the sanctification of the Spirit, for obedience to Jesus Christ and for sprinkling with his blood: May grace and peace be multiplied to you.

💬 Commentary

ABRAHAM BOOTH

Though justification and sanctification are both blessings of grace, and though they are inseparable, yet they are distinct acts of God; and there is, in various respects, a wide difference between them. The distinction may be thus expressed—justification respects the person in a legal sense, is a single act of grace, and terminates in a relative change; that is, a freedom from punishment, and a right to life; sanctification regards him in a physical sense, is a continual work of grace, and terminates in a real change, as to the quality both of habits and actions. The former is by a righteousness without us; the latter is by holiness wrought in us. That precedes as a cause; this follows as an effect. Justification is by Christ as a priest, and has regard to the guilt of sin; sanctification is by him as a king, and refers to its dominion. The former deprives of its damning power, the latter of its reigning power. Justification is instantaneous and complete in all its subjects; sanctification is progressive and perfecting by degrees.[39]

JOHN PIPER

Justification is the act of God by which he declares us to be just or righteous or perfect because by faith alone we have been united to Jesus Christ, who is perfect, who is just, who is righteous. So, justification is a legal standing before God, owing to a spiritual union with Jesus, which is owing to faith alone. You don't work yourself into or perform your way into this standing with God. He declares you to be perfect because of your union with Christ, and that happens by faith alone.

Sanctification is the act of God by which he, through his Spirit and his Word, is conforming you little by little—or in big steps—into the image of his Son. So we are really becoming in our behavior righteous, really overcoming imperfections in our sanctification.

Now here's the key question: How do these two relate to each other? The key verse is Hebrews 10:14: "By a single offering, [Christ] has perfected for all time those who are being sanctified." Think of what that says. Who has been perfected for all time? *Has been.* It's done. Has been perfected for all time. Those who are *being* perfected. Being sanctified. Being made holy. He has made you perfectly holy. Who? The ones who *are becoming* holy. Which means that the evidence that you stand holy or perfect or just before God is that you are by faith becoming holy. Sounds kind of paradoxical, I know. But it's the key to the Christian life.

Another way to say it is like this: The power by which you daily strive to overcome the imperfections in your life is the confidence that you're already perfect. If you get these switched around, if you think, "Okay, God demands perfection; I've got to become in my behavior perfect, and then God will look at me and say, 'He's doing pretty good; we'll let him be perfect or count him to be perfect.'" It's just the opposite. Because of Christ, we believe in him and what he did on the cross and his perfect life. We believe in him, and by that faith, God unites us to Christ. His perfection is counted as ours. And the evidence that we stand perfected in Christ is that we hate our sin, and we daily, by faith in his promises, strive to overcome the imperfections that exist.

So my exhortation would simply be, please don't get these backward. The whole world gets it all backward. Other religions get it all backward, where our works and our efforts to overcome imperfections might make us pleasing to God. You never can get there that way. God reckons us as acceptable, makes us his children, counts us as righteous; and because of that righteousness we then spend a lifetime becoming what we already are.

Prayer

Our Savior and Lord, you have completed the work of our justification. You have begun the work of our sanctification, and we trust that you will carry us through to its completion. Transform us day by day into your likeness, conforming us to your ways. Amen.

Question 33

Should those who have faith in Christ seek their salvation through their own works, or anywhere else?

No, they should not, as everything necessary to salvation is found in Christ. To seek salvation through good works is a denial that Christ is the only Redeemer and Savior.

📖 GALATIANS 2:16

Yet we know that a person is not justified by works of the law but through faith in Jesus Christ, so we also have believed in Christ Jesus, in order to be justified by faith in Christ and not by works of the law, because by works of the law no one will be justified.

🗩 Commentary

JOHN CALVIN

We maintain that of whatever kind a man's work may be, he is regarded as righteous before God simply on the ground of gratuitous mercy; because God, without any respect to works, freely adopts him in Christ, by imputing the righteousness of Christ to him as if it were his own. This we call the righteousness of faith, that is when a man, empty and drained of all confidence in works, feels convinced that the only ground of his acceptance with God is a righteousness which is wanting in himself, and is borrowed from Christ. The point on which the world goes astray (for this error has prevailed in almost every age), is in imagining that man, however partially defective he may be, still in some degree merits the favour of God by works. . . . God reconciles us to himself, from regard not to our works but to Christ alone, and by gratuitous adoption makes us his own children instead of children of wrath. So long as God regards our works, he finds no reason why he ought to love us. Wherefore it is necessary that he should bury our sins, impute to us the obedience of Christ which alone can stand his scrutiny, and adopt us as righteous through his merits. This is the clear and uniform doctrine of Scripture, "witnessed," as Paul says, "by the law and the prophets" (Rom. 3:21).[40]

TIMOTHY KELLER

If you mix faith and works, if you say, "Yes, I have to have faith in what Jesus has done for me, but I also have to add this or this or this, or I'm not saved," then you're saying that what actually saves you is not what Jesus has done, but what you add. It makes you your own savior.

This illustration might help. Mr. A asked Mr. B to make him a wooden cabinet because Mr. B was a great cabinetmaker. Mr. B and Mr. A were friends, and therefore Mr. B said, "Well, I better make this really good . . . perfect." So he worked and worked and worked on the cabinet till he got it to the place where it had been buffed and polished to perfection. He brought Mr. A into the workshop to see it, and Mr. A picked up a piece of sandpaper and said, "Let me just add one little stroke." Mr. B said, "No! It is finished. It's perfect. And there's no way to add to it without subtracting from it."

It's the same with Jesus Christ's work. Because when Jesus died, he said, "It is finished." There is nothing else to add to it. It's perfect. And if you add to it, you subtract from it. If you say, "He did this but I have to add this," anything you add becomes the real basis of your salvation and makes you your own savior.

The Protestant Reformers made strong biblical arguments that you cannot mix faith and works, that justification and righteousness and salvation must be through faith alone. I won't make any more of those arguments; I'll just say this: Personally, I couldn't live if that wasn't the case. I don't have any hope unless I can get up every day and stand on the bedrock knowledge that

> My hope is built on nothing less
> than Jesus' blood and righteousness.
> I dare not trust the sweetest frame
> but wholly lean on Jesus' name.[41]

That's my only hope.

🙏 Prayer

One and Only God, keep us from trusting in good works or living in such a way that we imply they are the grounds of our salvation. Let us glorify your grace by leaning our whole weight upon it, staking our lives on the promise that you are the beginning and the end of our salvation. Amen.

Question 34

Since we are redeemed by grace alone, through Christ alone, must we still do good works and obey God's Word?

Yes, because Christ, having redeemed us by his blood, also renews us by his Spirit; so that our lives may show love and gratitude to God; so that we may be assured of our faith by the fruits; and so that by our godly behavior others may be won to Christ.

📖 1 PETER 2:9–12

But you are a chosen race, a royal priesthood, a holy nation, a people for his own possession, that you may proclaim the excellencies of him who called you out of darkness into his marvelous light. Once you were not a people, but now you are God's people; once you had not received mercy, but now you have received mercy. Beloved, I urge you as sojourners and exiles to abstain from the passions of the flesh, which wage war against your soul. Keep your conduct among the Gentiles honorable, so that when they speak against you as evil-doers, they may see your good deeds and glorify God on the day of visitation.

⊟ Commentary

CHARLES HADDON SPURGEON

So, then, dear friends, these good works must be in the Christian. They are not the root, but the fruit of his salvation. They are not the way of the believer's salvation; they are his walk in the way of salvation. Where there is healthy life in a tree, the tree will bear fruit according to its kind; so, if God has made our nature good, the fruit will be good. But if the fruit be evil, it is because the tree is what it always was—an evil tree. The desire of men created anew in Christ is to be rid of every sin. We do sin, but we do not love sin. Sin gets power over us sometimes to our sorrow, but it is a kind of death to us to feel that we have gone into sin; yet it shall not have dominion over us, for we are not under the law, but under grace; and therefore we shall conquer it, and get the victory.[42]

LIGON DUNCAN

If salvation is by grace alone, through faith alone, in Christ alone—if we are saved and forgiven and accepted based not on our good works, not on our deserving, but on what Jesus has done for us—is there still a place for good works and obedience in the Christian life? The Bible gives an emphatic answer: yes.

First, there's a place for good works because, in salvation, we're saved not only from the penalty of sin, but also the power of sin. In salvation, through the work of Jesus Christ, we not only find forgive-ness, but we also find transformation. We are made new creations in Jesus Christ. He liberates us from the dominion of sin in our life. And so, salvation by grace does not mean that change or growth is unnecessary in the Christian life. It means that change and growth are now possible by God through his Holy Spirit working in us.

So what is the role of obedience to God's Word, of God's law in the Christian life? Gratitude, assurance, and witness.

In the Christian life all of our obedience is an act of gratitude to God for the grace that he has shown us in Jesus Christ. Remember what Paul says in Ephesians 2: "For by grace you have been saved through faith. And this is not your own doing; it is the gift of God, not a result of works, so that no one may boast. For we are his workmanship, created in Christ Jesus for good works" (vv. 8–10). Now, did you hear what Paul said there? He didn't say that we were saved *by* good works. In fact, he explicitly excluded that. But he did say that we were saved *to* good works, *for* good works. So the role of works in the Christian life is not to save us. It's not to get God to love us. It's to express our gratitude to God for the prior love that he's shown us in Jesus Christ and for the salvation that he's freely given us in Jesus Christ. And so all of our obedience to God's Word in the Christian life is an act of gratitude.

Second, good works done in faith also serve to assure us. In his first letter to the Thessalonians, Paul explains that he knows that they are the chosen of God (1 Thess. 1:3–5). Now that's a striking thing to say. How would you know people are chosen of God? In verse 3, Paul speaks of the Thessalonians' works of faith, their labor of love, and their patience of hope. He's essentially saying, "I see the work of the Holy Spirit in your life, and that lets me know that you are the children of God." And then he explains how that serves their own assurance (v. 5). We are given assurance in the Christian life when we see God at work in us to change us, and that's expressed in our obeying God's commands.

A third way that the law works in the Christian life and that good works and obedience work in the Christian life, is in the area of witness. When we obey the Word of God, when we do good works, we glorify our heavenly Father. And those who see us are given reason to glorify our heavenly Father. Peter explains that when he says that he wants us to live godly lives quietly before the world so that the world will look at us and glorify our loving heavenly Father who saved us by grace (1 Pet. 2:12).

So, though we're saved by grace, we're saved to a life of joyful good works and obedience. Not to get God to love us, but because God does love us, and we want to be like his Son, who said, "My food is to do the will of him who sent me" (John 4:34).

✋ Prayer

Heavenly Father, you have saved us *from* sin. Let us not continue in it as if we were still enslaved to it. You have given us commands that are the path of life. Let us treasure those commands. May all who know us see our good works and glorify you because of them. Amen.

Question 35

Since we are redeemed by grace alone, through faith alone, where does this faith come from?

All the gifts we receive from Christ we receive through the Holy Spirit, including faith itself.

📖 TITUS 3:4–6

But when the goodness and loving kindness of God our Savior appeared, he saved us, not because of works done by us in righteousness, but according to his own mercy, by the washing of regeneration and renewal of the Holy Spirit, whom he poured out on us richly through Jesus Christ our Savior.

💬 Commentary

FRANCIS SCHAEFFER

We must realize that Christianity is the easiest religion in the world, because it is the only religion in which God the Father and Christ and the Holy Spirit do everything. God is the Creator; we have nothing to do with our existence, or the existence of other things. We can shape other things, but we cannot change the fact of existence. We do nothing for our salvation because Christ did it all. We do not have to do anything. In every other religion we have to do something . . . but with Christianity we do not do anything; God has done it all: He has created us and He has sent His Son; His Son died and because the Son is infinite, therefore he bears our total guilt. We do not need to bear our guilt, nor do we even have to merit the merit of Christ. He does it all. So in one way it is the easiest religion in the world.[43]

MIKA EDMONDSON

This question deals with how believers come to faith and so receive the salvation purchased by Christ. It's a question best asked in retrospect, as we look back over our lives and ask, "How did I, a fallen sinner, come to love Jesus and believe his gospel where so many others have not?"

In order to understand the magnitude of this, you have to understand that "the word of the cross is folly to those who are perishing" (1 Cor. 1:18). Although we can intellectually comprehend the facts of the gospel, apart from the gracious intervention of God, we would reject it as folly. But the catechism reminds us that God does intervene. The Holy Spirit gives new life to sinners who were otherwise "dead in trespasses and sins" (Eph. 2:1). As the gospel is preached, the Holy Spirit creates faith in our hearts so that we embrace the risen and reigning Christ as he presents himself through the gospel. Even faith (our obedient response to the gospel) is a gracious gift of God. This amazing truth has huge implications for how we view our salvation, the Christian life, and worship.

First, it confirms that our salvation is truly all of grace. None of us can boast that we're saved because we made the most of the salvation offered to us. We certainly aren't saved because we had enough moral and spiritual sense in and of ourselves to believe the gospel or because we were catechized so well (although that is important). No, we are saved only because, in his divine compassion, the risen Christ gave us the spiritual sight to believe the gospel. By his Holy Spirit, Jesus tilled the rocky soil of our hearts so that as the seed of the gospel was sown, it would bring forth the fruit of faith and repentance. If we believe the gospel, we should praise God for giving us the grace to believe it, for he is the only One who made the difference for us. Therefore, the Christian life must be marked by gratitude and humility. In and of ourselves, we are no better than our non-Christian neighbors. The only difference is that something (or, rather, someone) absolutely wonderful has come into our lives and changed everything.

Finally, knowing that our faith is a gift of God changes how we view public worship, particularly the preaching of the gospel. Through gospel proclamation, the risen Christ presents himself in saving power and transforms people for eternity. Eternal life does not begin when Christ returns; eternal life begins today as the Holy Spirit brings that life to us through the gospel, the power of God unto salvation. As we sit in our pews hearing the gospel, we are not just listening to a religious lecture. The greatest power in all the world is at work bringing new life to sinners. Heaven is coming to earth, a glorious "not yet" is breaking into the "here and now." Public worship is the center of God's redemptive action until Christ's return when the world will behold him. Until that time, we behold him by faith, week by week, as we gather together in his name to worship him and hear his Word. And by the Holy Spirit, we are progressively being transformed in a way that will last for eternity.

Prayer

Holy Spirit, you sought us when we could not seek you because we were dead in our trespasses and sins. You are the giver of our faith; none of us would believe apart from your regenerating grace, by which you make hearts of stone into hearts of flesh. Let us put aside all boasting in light of your undeserved mercy. Amen.

Part 3

Spirit, Restoration, Growing in Grace

Question 36

What do we believe
about the Holy Spirit?

That he is God, coeternal with the Father and the Son, and that God
grants him irrevocably to all who believe.

📖 JOHN 14:16–17

And I will ask the Father, and he will give you another Helper, to be
with you forever, even the Spirit of truth, whom the world cannot
receive, because it neither sees him nor knows him. You know him,
for he dwells with you and will be in you.

💬 Commentary

AUGUSTINE OF HIPPO

Wherefore, when our Lord breathed on His disciples, and said, "Receive ye the Holy Ghost," He certainly wished it to be understood
that the Holy Ghost was not only the Spirit of the Father, but of the
only begotten Son Himself. For the same Spirit is, indeed, the Spirit
of the Father and of the Son, making with them the trinity of Father,
Son, and Spirit, not a creature, but the Creator.[44]

SAM STORMS

Rarely does a Christian struggle to think of God as Father. And to envision God as Son is not a problem for many. These personal names come easily to us because our lives and relationships are inescapably intertwined with fathers and sons here on earth. But God as Holy Spirit is often a different matter. Gordon Fee tells of one of his students who remarked, "God the Father makes perfectly good sense to me, and God the Son I can quite understand; but the Holy Spirit is a gray, oblong blur."[45]

How different this is from what we actually read in Scripture. There we see that the Spirit is not third in rank in the Godhead but is coequal and coeternal with the Father and Son, sharing with them all the glory and honor due unto our triune God. The Holy Spirit is not an impersonal power or an ethereal, abstract energy. The Spirit is personal in every sense of the term. He has a mind and thinks (Isa. 11:2; Rom. 8:27). He is capable of experiencing deep affections and feelings (Rom. 8:26; 15:30). The Spirit has a will and makes choices regarding what is best for God's people and what will most glorify the Son (Acts 16:7; 1 Cor. 2:11).

We see even more of the Spirit's personality when he is described as being grieved when we sin (Eph. 4:30). The Spirit, no less so than the Father and the Son, enters into a vibrant and intimate relationship with all whom he indwells (2 Cor. 13:14). The Spirit talks (Mark 13:11; Rev. 2:7), testifies (John 15:26; 16:13) encourages (Acts 9:31), strengthens (Eph. 3:16), and teaches us, especially in times of spiritual emergency (Luke 12:12). That the Spirit is personal is seen in that he can be lied to (Acts 5:3), insulted (Heb. 10:29), and even blasphemed (Matt. 12:31–32).

Above all else, though, the Holy Spirit is the "Spirit of Christ" (Rom. 8:9). His primary role in us, the temple of God in whom he dwells (Eph. 2:21–22), is other-directed or other-oriented as he ministers to direct our attention to the person of Christ and to awaken in us heartfelt affection for and devotion to the Savior (John 14:26; 16:12–15). The Holy Spirit delights above all else in serving as a spotlight, standing behind us (although certainly dwelling within us) to focus our thoughts and meditation on the beauty of Christ and all that God is for us in and through him.

As we prayerfully meditate on the person and work of the Spirit and give thanks for his powerful presence in our lives, we would do well to consider the words of Thomas Torrance, who reminds us that "the Spirit is not just something divine or something akin to God emanating from him, not some sort of action at a distance or some kind of gift detachable from himself, for in the Holy Spirit God acts directly upon us himself, and in giving us his Holy Spirit God gives us nothing less than himself."[46]

Prayer

God Our Help, we thank you for sending your Spirit to live in us. Thank you that he chastens and disciplines, strengthens and comforts us. Let us live the life of faith in his power, not our own. Let us walk the path of obedience, filled with his joy. Amen.

Question 37

How does the Holy
Spirit help us?

The Holy Spirit convicts us of our sin, comforts us, guides us, gives
us spiritual gifts and the desire to obey God; and he enables us to
pray and to understand God's Word.

📖 EPHESIANS 6:17–18

And take the helmet of salvation, and the sword of the Spirit, which
is the word of God, praying at all times in the Spirit, with all prayer
and supplication. To that end keep alert with all perseverance, making
supplication for all the saints.

💬 Commentary

JOHN OWEN

The Holy Spirit dwelling in us gives guidance and direction. Funda-
mentally, habitually, he enlightens our minds, give us eyes, under-
standings, shines into us, translates us from darkness into marvelous
light, whereby we are able to see our way, to know our paths, and to
discern the things of God. . . . He gives a new light and understanding,

whereby, in general, we are enabled to "discern, comprehend, and receive spiritual things." . . . Strength comes as well as light, by the pouring out of the Spirit on us; strength for the receiving and practice of all his gracious discoveries to us. . . . From this indwelling of the Spirit we have supportment. Our hearts are very ready to sink and fail under our trials; indeed, a little thing will cause us so to do: flesh, and heart, and all that is within us, are soon ready to fail. . . . The Spirit helpeth, bears up that infirmity which is ready to make us go double.[47]

LEO SCHUSTER

I've always been struck by Jesus's words: "Apart from me you can do nothing." They are a humbling and refreshing reminder that our need, from first to last, isn't partial, but total. By giving us the Holy Spirit, Christ has given us all we need and more, from first to last. The Holy Spirit gives us life. He fills our life and points us to the One who is life. He gives us life in that our starting point is not simply that we're spiritually needy, but that we are dead in sin. Our spiritual life begins when the Holy Spirit regenerates us, giving us new life. When he turns our heart of stone into a heart of flesh, he makes the truth of God's Word real to us, and we freely embrace Christ as he's offered to us in the gospel. This reminds us that being a Christian isn't about being a better person but about being a new person, by God's grace alone, through faith alone.

Not only does he give us life, but he also fills our life. When we become Christians, God the Father adopts us as his children and gives to us his Spirit of adoption. He comes to live in us and fill us, and in doing so he guides us as a counselor would—supporting, convicting us of our sin, strengthening us in Christ, encouraging us in the way we should live, helping us to pray, and even praying for us when we're too weak to do so ourselves. In all this, he grows us in Christlikeness, enabling us to do good works, which God has prepared in advance for us to do. And he gives us specific gifts to use to contribute to the building up of the body of Christ, and to love, serve, and obey God.

So he gives us life. He fills our life. And finally, he points us to the

One who is life. Jesus said, "[The Spirit] will glorify me, for he will take what is mine and declare it to you" (John 16:14). The Holy Spirit is the Spirit of Christ. He doesn't draw attention to himself but glorifies Jesus and gives us the grace to do the same, making him who is life our life and love. So the One who is the Alpha and Omega, the First and the Last, has given us his Spirit to supply all we need from first to last. He gives us life, fills our life, and points us to the One who is life.

✋ Prayer

God the Spirit, have your way in us. Shine your light on the secret sins of our hearts. Equip us for tasks that are too large for us. Make us glad in what delights you. Intercede for us and open our eyes to rightly understand the Word of truth. Amen.

Question 38

What is prayer?

Prayer is pouring out our hearts to God in praise, petition, confession of sin, and thanksgiving.

📖 PSALM 62:8

Trust in him at all times, O people; pour out your heart before him; God is a refuge for us.

💬 Commentary

ABRAHAM BOOTH

As the enemies of your soul are inveterate, subtle, and powerful, and your spiritual frames inconstant, it is highly necessary you should live under a continual remembrance of those awakening considerations. What more advisable, what so necessary for you, as to walk circumspectly; to watch and pray, lest you enter into temptation? A sense of your own weakness and insufficiency, should ever abide on your mind and appear in your conduct. As the corruption of nature is an enemy that is always near you, and always in you, while on earth; and as it is very strongly disposed to second every temptation from without; you should "keep your heart with all diligence." Watch, diligently watch, over all its imaginations, motions, and tendencies. Consider whence they arise and to what they incline, before you execute any of the purposes formed in it. For such is the superlative deceitfulness of the human heart, "that he who trusteth in it is a fool," ignorant of his danger, and unmindful of his best interests. This consideration should cause every child of God to bend the suppliant knee, with the utmost frequency, humility, and fervour: to live, as it were, at the throne of grace; nor depart thence till far from the reach of danger. Certain it is, that the more we see of the strength of our adversaries and of the danger we are in from them, the more shall we exercise ourselves in fervent prayer. Can you, O Christian, be cool and indifferent, be dull and careless, when the world, the flesh, and the devil are your implacable and unwearied opposers?[48]

JOHN PIPER

Prayer is the way you walk by the Spirit. Prayer is the way you walk by faith. In other words, it's the breath of the Christian life all day long. Just breathe in, breathe out. It's the way you live.

Let me illustrate for you with four elements from the catechism: confession, petition, praise, and thanks. I'm commending to you that any time you face any situation when you feel *I need help here*, you do it by prayer using these four elements.

Suppose I have to speak in front of a group, and I am nervous (you can pick your particular challenge). As the moment approaches, I wonder, "Am I going to be able to do this? Will I remember what I have to say? Will I make a fool of myself?" And at that moment I *confess* my need to God. I say, "Lord, I'm a sinner. I don't deserve your help, but I need your help. I can't do anything without you." That's the *confession* step of prayer.

And then I turn my confession to *petition*. "Lord, please help me. I need memory. I need articulation. I need the right spirit. I need humility. I need to look the people in the eye. I need all these things. I want to be helpful to my listeners. But I don't have it in me to be all that they need. Help me." That's the *petition* step of prayer. A cry for help.

And then I need to reach out and take hold of something about God that will be worthy of my praise and worthy of my trust. Like God says, "I'll strengthen you. I'll help you. I'll hold you up with my victorious right hand" (see Isa. 41:10). I take hold of that promise, that power, that love, that mercy, and I hold onto it. And I *trust him and praise him.* "You, oh Lord, can help me. I trust you to help me. I praise you for being the kind of God who is willing and able to help me!" That's the *trust* and *praise* step of prayer.

Then I give my talk, trusting him. And when I am done, no matter what, I thank him. Since I trusted him for his help, I believe that he is going to use my effort, no matter how well I think I did. "Thank you, Lord!" That is the *thanks* step of prayer.

There they are—four key words from the catechism.

First, continually *confess* your need to the Lord. "I need you."

Second, cry out in *petition.* "Help me."

Third, lay hold of God's promises with trust and *praise* for his ability to fulfill them.

And then when he helps you, go on your face and say, "*Thank* you."

That's the rhythm and the breath of the Christian life.

Prayer

Our Great Refuge, thank you for calling us to prayer. You are not far away; you are near, and you hear us when we pray. Let us pour out our hearts to you without ceasing. Let us pray without guile, bringing our true selves before your throne of grace. Amen.

Question 39

With what attitude should we pray?

With love, perseverance, and gratefulness; in humble submission to God's will, knowing that, for the sake of Christ, he always hears our prayers.

📖 PHILIPPIANS 4:6

Do not be anxious about anything, but in everything by prayer and supplication with thanksgiving let your requests be made known to God.

💬 Commentary

JOHN BUNYAN

Before you enter into prayer, ask thy soul these questions: To what end, O my soul, art thou retired into this place? Art thou not come to discourse the Lord in prayer? Is he present; will he hear thee? Is he merciful; will he help thee? Is thy business slight; is it not concerning the welfare of thy soul? What words wilt thou use to move him to compassion? To make thy preparation complete, consider that thou art but dust and ashes, and he the great God, Father of our Lord Jesus Christ, that clothes himself with light as with a garment; that thou art a vile sinner, he a holy God; that thou art but a poor crawling worm, he the omnipotent Creator. In all your prayers forget not to thank the Lord for his mercies. When thou prayest, rather let thy heart be without words, than thy words without a heart. Prayer will make a man cease from sin, or sin will entice a man to cease from prayer.[49]

THABITI ANYABWILE

Hypocritical prayer is an oxymoron; hypocrisy and prayer just don't go together. Anything that we properly call prayer should be divorced from hypocrisy. The Lord teaches us this in the Gospels when he talks about those who pray for an audience; for them prayer is a show. And if you've been praying any length of time, you know that you don't need an audience for your prayers to be a show. Sometimes we're watching ourselves pray. We're admiring the eloquence of our appeal. We like the turn of phrase. So our prayer can go from being an act of communion with God to a demonstration of pride.

But real prayer is an expression of love. Real prayer is an expression of perseverance. It's an expression of gratefulness.

Why love? Because in prayer we're communing with God the Father, God the Son, God the Holy Spirit. We're praying to the Father in the name of the Son through the Spirit. And in the act of prayer, we're meant to enjoy them and to get to know them and to commune with them. How can prayer be communion without love?

In prayer there should also be perseverance, steadfastness, pressing in, continuously knocking at the door. This perseverance is necessary to prevail against our flesh. Our flesh wars against the spirit. And, boy, I tell you, when we pray, don't we sometimes experience a wandering, distracting mind? When we pray, don't we sometimes experience our frailty, our weakness, our fatigue? I've fallen asleep praying just as our Lord's apostles did in the garden of Gethsemane. So we need perseverance, and we need that pressing into the things of God, that pushing out the distractions of the world, that crucifying of the flesh, again, that we might have this fuller communion with the Lord.

Finally, prayer ought to be an expression of gratitude. Let us count the blessings of the Lord. Let us mark his providences. Let us observe the divine interruptions that have broken into our lives, such that we might receive not only Christ but everything in Christ, and receive and experience it in surprising ways, in opportune times, in times later than we had hoped for or expected. The divine interruptions of God, which are blessings and distributions of his kindness to us, ought to cultivate gratitude in us. Our prayers ought to express that gratitude so that we're conscious of the kindness and goodness of the Lord.

Even when we can't trace God's hand, as the saying goes, we can trust his heart because we know God is good, and we're grateful for his goodness. That spurs us on in our prayer and perseverance, and it turns us again in love toward Christ our Savior, God our Father, and the Spirit our Comforter.

Prayer

Loving Father, we come to you in the name of your beloved Son. Give us perseverance in prayer, even when we do not immediately see answers. Let us believe that you will not keep back any good thing from us, and trust that you will withhold those things we seek that would harm us. Your ways are higher than our ways, and we entrust our requests to your sovereign kindness. Amen.

Question 40

What should we pray?

The whole Word of God directs and inspires us in what we should pray, including the prayer Jesus himself taught us.

📖 EPHESIANS 3:14–21

For this reason I bow my knees before the Father, from whom every family in heaven and on earth is named, that according to the riches of his glory he may grant you to be strengthened with power through his Spirit in your inner being, so that Christ may dwell in your hearts through faith—that you, being rooted and grounded in love, may have strength to comprehend with all the saints what is the breadth and length and height and depth, and to know the love of Christ that surpasses knowledge, that you may be filled with all the fullness of God.

Now to him who is able to do far more abundantly than all that we ask or think, according to the power at work within us, to him be glory in the church and in Christ Jesus throughout all generations, forever and ever. Amen.

⊟ Commentary

JOHN CHRYSOSTOM

Great is the profit to be derived from the sacred Scriptures and their assistance is sufficient for every need. Paul was pointing this out when he said, "Whatever things have been written have been written for our instruction, upon whom the final age of the world has come, that through the patience and the consolation afforded by the Scriptures we may have hope." (Rom. 15:4; see 1 Cor. 10:11) The divine words, indeed, are a treasury containing every sort of remedy, so that, whether one needs to put down senseless pride, or to quench the fire of concupiscence or to trample on the love of riches, or to despise pain, or to cultivate cheerfulness and acquire patience—in them one may find in abundance the means to do so.[50]

ALISTAIR BEGG

When we're asking what we should pray about, we instinctively turn to the Bible, because it's the Bible that inspires us and directs us. So whether it's Jesus reminding us that we should always pray and not faint or Paul reminding the Philippians not to be anxious about anything but in everything to turn to God in prayer, it is the Bible that keeps us on track. As we pray, we're really asking God to bring our lives and the lives of others into line with his purposes. And when we pray in that way, we're able to pray with confidence.

So, we can pray for our world, that men and women might come to believe the gospel. We can pray for laborers to be sent into the harvest field, as Jesus said. We can pray for the work of the gospel in our own lives, that we might become holy and joyful and thankful. And when we do all of this, we need to remember that God is far more willing to bless us than we are even to take the time to ask him.

As Jesus said, "If you then, who are evil, know how to give good gifts to your children, how much more will your Father who is in heaven give good things to those who ask him!" (Matt. 7:11).

✍ Prayer

God Who Hears, let your living Word shape our desires and our prayers. May it challenge us to pray for things that don't seem possible. May it inform our view of you as we approach you as beloved sons and daughters. May it drive us to our knees as we recognize our need of you. Amen.

.

What is the Lord's Prayer?

Our Father in heaven, hallowed be your name, your kingdom come, your will be done, on earth as it is in heaven. Give us today our daily bread. And forgive us our debts, as we also have forgiven our debtors. And lead us not into temptation, but deliver us from evil.

📖 MATTHEW 6:9

Pray then like this: "Our Father in heaven, hallowed be your name. . . ."

💬 Commentary

MARTIN LUTHER

Do you, however, feel weak and timid? for flesh and blood always hinder faith, as if you were not worthy or fit and in earnest to pray; or do you doubt whether God has heard you, because you are a sinner? then cling to the word and say: Though I am a sinner and unworthy, yet I have the command of God, that tells me to pray, and his promise that he will graciously hear me, not because of my worthiness, but for the sake of the Lord Christ. By this means you can drive away the thoughts and doubts, and cheerfully kneel down and pray, not regarding your worthiness or unworthiness, but your need and his word upon which he tells you to build; especially since he has placed before you and put into your mouth the words how and what you are to pray for, so that you joyously send up these prayers through him, and can lay them in his bosom, that he may lay them by his own worthiness before the Father.[51]

JUAN SANCHEZ

When Jesus's disciples asked him to teach them to pray, Jesus gave them a model prayer. We call it the Lord's Prayer, but really it's the Lord's model prayer. It is the way Jesus taught his disciples to pray.

When we say, "Our Father," we remember that the God who created the universe is our Father in heaven. He is the Father who provides. He is the Father who sustains. He is the Father who protects. And the prayer reminds us that we are able to run to our Father to let our needs be known.

But Jesus also reminded us that he's not only our Father but he's also our King. So when we say, "Your kingdom come, your will be done," we realize our Father is the King. We're coming to our Father, who is the King of the universe, who has complete and total authority over all things. Our focus must first and foremost be on our Father, who is King. And the greatest joy for his children is that his name would be hallowed, that his name would be famous. And so we should pray, "God, make your name famous." The Lord's Prayer is also a corporate prayer. "*Our* Father" reminds us that we're not an only child. Our desire is to make sure his name is hallowed over all the earth. Ultimately, this world is not our home, and we long for his kingdom to finally and fully be established. But until then, Jesus reminded us that we can go to our Father. When we fail our Father, when we fail our King, we can ask for forgiveness.

The Lord's model prayer instructs us that we are utterly dependent upon our Father for all of our daily needs. I think modern-day people tend to forget this. Jesus said to pray in this way: "Give us *this* day our *daily* bread." That is very humbling.

Finally, until God's kingdom comes we need to understand that we are engaged in a spiritual battle, and we need protection. We ask our King to protect us. In fact, the apostle Paul reminds us that in this spiritual warfare that we don't put on *our* armor, we put on God's armor (Eph. 6:10–18). We put on our King's armor. We put on our Father's armor, and we fight in the strength of our Father. So it is right and good for us—whatever our needs or circumstances may be—to remember that we are utterly dependent, moment by moment, breath by breath, on our Father King, and we can run to him. We can come to him, and we can ask him for the things that we need.

As long as we have breath in us, let us live to make the King's name famous, to hallow his name, both as a church and also as individual Christians, longing for his kingdom to come. Let us long for the return of Jesus, but know that until that day comes, he will pardon our sin, he will provide our daily bread, and he will protect us from the Evil One.

✍ Prayer

Our Father in Heaven, when we pray the prayer that you taught us, keep us from reciting empty words. Let these petitions be the cries of our hearts. Bring your kingdom on earth to us and through us for your great name's sake. Amen.

Question 42

How is the Word of God to be read and heard?

With diligence, preparation, and prayer; so that we may accept it with faith, store it in our hearts, and practice it in our lives.

📖 2 TIMOTHY 3:16–17

All Scripture is breathed out by God and profitable for teaching, for reproof, for correction, and for training in righteousness, that the man of God may be complete, equipped for every good work.

💬 Commentary

THOMAS CRANMER

Wherefore I would advise you all that come to the reading or hearing of this book, which is the word of God, the most precious jewel and most holy relic that remaineth upon earth; that ye bring with you the fear of God, and that ye do it with all due reverence, and use your knowledge thereof, not to vain glory of frivolous disputation, but to the honor of God, increase of virtue, and edification both of yourselves and others.[52]

KEVIN DEYOUNG

The Bible is not just another book, and so we ought to approach it in a unique way. The Bible is God-breathed: "All Scripture is breathed out by God" (2 Tim. 3:16). It's inspired. That doesn't mean that the Bible is inspiring. Now, it *is* inspiring. But whether anyone in the world is inspired by the Bible, the Bible is still inspired itself. It's God's Word to us. It's God exhaling, God opening his most hallowed lips and speaking to us. So, this Word is God's Word, and this Word is exactly what God wanted to be written down in Holy Scriptures.

That means we ought to approach Scripture with a special reverence and with special care. We come to the Bible very carefully. We want to be diligent. We want to be prepared. We want to take it seriously. And we also come to this book with a special reverence, because God is speaking to us. One of the ways to think of submitting to the Word is that we stop telling God what to do. God now speaks to us. A theologian once said that to be a Christian means you put your hand over your mouth and are silent. This doesn't mean that we can't ever cry out to God. Certainly the Psalms are full of that. But it means that we approach Scripture with reverence, wanting to hear from God, submitting ourselves fully to the Word of God.

When we come to the Bible, our aim is not just information. It's never less than information—we're not against information. God uses that. But it's more than just information we're trying to get from the Bible. We want faith. That's what God wants: for us to accept the Word with faith, with a real delight, with a desire for it, a dependence upon it.

When we embrace God's Word with faith, we store it up in our hearts. Charles Spurgeon said of John Bunyan that if you would prick him, his blood would be bibline. He was so full of the Scriptures that it came out of him. That's what we want; that's why we store it up.

And then we practice it. Did Jesus say, "If you love me, you will have a tingling sensation in your heart"? No, he didn't say that, though that's wonderful. But he said, "If you love me, *you will keep my commandments"* (John 14:15). So if we are serious about loving God, we must be very serious about obeying God and obeying his Word to us. That's the aim: to be transformed by it, to embrace it in faith, and to worship at his feet.

Really, in its simplest form, we ought to come to the Word of God with the same sort of attitude with which we'd come to God himself. If God spoke to you, which he does in the Scriptures, if God opened his mouth to us, how would we approach him? Well, I think we would listen carefully. We would listen diligently. We would listen submissively. We would listen expectantly. And we'd listen with an aim to love and obey.

Prayer

Giver of the Word, help us to treasure your Scriptures as our most precious possession. May it be in our minds and on our lips. Let it transform our thinking and reform our living. Make us attentive students and devoted servants of your perfect Word. Amen.

Question 43

What are the sacraments or ordinances?

The sacraments or ordinances given by God and instituted by Christ, namely baptism and the Lord's Supper, are visible signs and seals that we are bound together as a community of faith by his death and resurrection. By our use of them the Holy Spirit more fully declares and seals the promises of the gospel to us.

📖 ROMANS 6:4

We were buried therefore with him by baptism into death, in order that, just as Christ was raised from the dead by the glory of the Father, we too might walk in newness of life.

📖 LUKE 22:19–20

And he took bread, and when he had given thanks, he broke it and gave it to them, saying, "This is my body, which is given for you. Do this in remembrance of me." And likewise the cup after they had eaten, saying, "This cup that is poured out for you is the new covenant in my blood."

💬 Commentary

CHARLES SIMEON

So say I of baptism and of the Lord's Supper: "In their proper and appointed use they cannot be too highly valued: but, if abused to purposes for which they were not given, and looked to as containing in themselves, and conveying of themselves, salvation to man, they are desecrated." . . . Let us learn, then, from hence, how to use God's ordinances—We should be thankful for them: we should honour them: we should look to God in them, and expect from God through them the communications of his grace and peace. They are to be reverenced, but not idolized; to be used as means, but not rested in as an end. No one is to imagine himself the better, merely because he has attended on any ordinances.[53]

TIMOTHY KELLER

There are two sacraments or ordinances. There's baptism, which is once for all. And there's the Lord's Supper, which is ongoing and regular. We call both of them *ordinances* because Jesus Christ commands us to do them. But we call them *sacraments* because through them God's blessing and grace come to us in unique ways. They are not just personal, individual experiences. We are members of a community, and baptism and the Lord's Supper show that we belong to that community, the covenant community, the people who belong to Jesus. And that's the reason why these are actually like boundary markers. The Westminster Confession says they "put a visible difference between those that belong to the church and the rest of the world."[54]

They are both signs and seals. We call them *signs* because they symbolize the blessings of salvation, forgiveness for sins, reception of the Holy Spirit, and the ability to commune with Jesus Christ in his presence. But they're not only signs; they're also *seals*. That means they actually bring these blessings to us. They assure us and stir up our faith, and it's our faith that receives those blessings.

Some places in the Bible, such as 1 Corinthians 10 and 1 Peter 3, seem to say that it's the sacraments that actually receive the blessings of salvation. But the sacraments stir up our faith, and our faith is what actually receives the blessings and what saves us. So J. I. Packer puts it like this: "As the preaching of the Word makes the gospel audible, so the sacraments make it visible, and God stirs up faith by both means."[55] Sacraments, therefore, function as a means of grace on the principle that, literally, seeing leads to believing.

Prayer

Giver of the Gospel, you have given us signs of your grace that can be seen, felt, and tasted. Help us to observe them according to your commands. May they turn our eyes away from ourselves and onto your saving work. Keep us from exalting the signs in any way that distracts us from the Savior to which they point. Amen.

Question 44

What is baptism?

Baptism is the washing with water in the name of the Father, the Son, and the Holy Spirit; it signifies and seals our adoption into Christ, our cleansing from sin, and our commitment to belong to the Lord and to his church.

📖 MATTHEW 28:19

Go therefore and make disciples of all nations, baptizing them in the name of the Father and of the Son and of the Holy Spirit. . . .

💬 Commentary

GEORGE HERBERT

> As he that sees a dark and shady grove,
> Stays not, but looks beyond it on the sky
> So when I view my sins, mine eyes remove
> More backward still, and to that water fly,
> Which is above the heav'ns, whose spring and rent
> Is in my dear Redeemer's pierced side.
> O blessed streams! either ye do prevent
> And stop our sins from growing thick and wide,

191

Or else give tears to drown them, as they grow.
In you Redemption measures all my time,
And spreads the plaster equal to the crime:
You taught the book of life my name, that so,
Whatever future sins should me miscall,
Your first acquaintance might discredit all.[56]

COLLIN HANSEN

When I told my pastor I wanted to become a church member, he offered a simple explanation for why I should then seek baptism: because Jesus did so. Why, though, did Jesus wade into the Jordan and ask his cousin John to lower him beneath the waters? After all, he had no sin to confess, no need to repent.

I've always sympathized with John's incredulous response to Jesus's request. "I need to be baptized by you," said John, who prepared the way for the Christ, "and do you come to me?" (Matt. 3:14).

Yes, Jesus responded, "for thus it is fitting for us to fulfill all righteousness" (Matt. 3:15).

In his baptism, Jesus identified with all of us who, because of sin, will someday die as a result of God's judgment (Gen. 3:19). Water has been a sign of God's judgment since Genesis 6–7, when God judged the wickedness of man and sent a flood to destroy all but Noah and his family. Though he never would sin, Jesus would nevertheless die at the hands of sinful men as he absorbed the wrath of God for the sinful world.

Water, of course, is also necessary for life. Before there was light, the Spirit of God hovered over the waters (Gen. 1:2). And one day when the resurrected and ascended Jesus returns to inaugurate the new heavens and the new earth, a river of life will flow from the throne of God and of the Lamb in the New Jerusalem (Rev. 22:1–2). Any who follow him into the waves as enemies of God will emerge as brothers and sisters of the Son of God, fellow heirs of his eternal inheritance.

Baptism is a sign and seal that we have been adopted into the family of God. Father, Son, and Holy Spirit have loved one another in perfect unity since before creation, before God molded Adam from the dust. At Jesus's baptism we notice all three persons. As Jesus emerges from the water, the Spirit of God descends like a dove and rests on him (Matt 3:16). So that no one will mistake the meaning of the sign, the Father boasts from heaven, "This is my beloved Son, with whom I am well pleased" (Matt. 3:17).

Every time I remember my baptism, I hear these words of blessing. Jesus was plunged beneath the waters of judgment, so that I might drink the waters of everlasting life. Because Jesus calls me brother, I can call God my Father. Because the Spirit descended on him as a dove, I have peace with God, who once regarded me as his enemy.

Once I was outside the people of God, estranged from this family due to my sin. But now I am a brother to all who have been likewise baptized in the name of the Father, Son, and Holy Spirit. The church is our home, the place where, despite our disagreements and disputes, we come together to confess that we have one Lord and one faith (Eph. 4:5). To us has been given the Great Commission to follow in John's footsteps and call others to repentance while we point them to Jesus, the Lamb of God who takes away the sin of the world (John 1:29). We baptize so they might always know that God loves them, that he is well pleased with them because they now belong to Christ.

Prayer

Cleansing One, we cannot purify our own hearts, but must come to you to wash away our sin. Thank you for water baptism, which does not save us but portrays our salvation and unites us as one people, your adopted sons and daughters. Amen.

Is baptism with water the washing away of sin itself?

No, only the blood of Christ and the renewal of the Holy Spirit can cleanse us from sin.

LUKE 3:16

John answered them all, saying, "I baptize you with water, but he who is mightier than I is coming, the strap of whose sandals I am not worthy to untie. He will baptize you with the Holy Spirit and fire."

Commentary

JOHN CALVIN

"He shall baptize you with the Holy Spirit and with fire." It is asked, why did not John equally say, that it is Christ alone who washes souls with his blood? The reason is, that this very washing is performed by the power of the Spirit, and John reckoned it enough to express the whole effect of baptism by the single word Spirit. The meaning is clear, that Christ alone bestows all the grace which is figuratively represented by outward baptism, because it is he who "sprinkles the conscience" with his blood. It is he also who mortifies the old man, and bestows the Spirit of regeneration. The word fire is added as an epithet, and is applied to the Spirit, because he takes away our pollutions, as fire purifies gold.[57]

R. KENT HUGHES

The great classic text that celebrates and announces the believer's baptism into Christ is 1 Corinthians 12:13: "For in one Spirit we were all baptized into one body—Jews or Greeks, slaves or free—and all were made to drink of one Spirit." That speaks of the Spirit's initiating us into the body of Christ, and that happened to me when I was just twelve years old. I'd never heard of the baptism of the Holy Spirit, but I was indeed baptized by the Holy Spirit. And now as the years have gone by, what was an objective fact has become a subjective reality in my life.

When I was baptized by the Spirit, I was regenerated, born again. I was born of the Spirit, John 3 says. What a beautiful picture. The metaphor of being born again describes a divine obstetrics because I was taken out of darkness and I was brought into light, and I began to see things.

At the same time I was regenerated, I was indwelled by the Holy Spirit. Jesus says in John 14 that the Spirit "will live with you" and "will be in you." I lost my father when I was a little boy and had a sense of being alone in this world. When I became indwelt, a sense of paternity overtook my soul, of being adopted. I didn't know that I'd been tagged by the Holy Spirit or sealed by the Holy Spirit. As it says in Ephesians 1:13–14: "In him you also, when you heard the word of truth, the gospel of your salvation, and believed in him, were sealed with the promised Holy Spirit, who is the guarantee of our inheritance until we acquire possession of it, to the praise of his glory." That further gave me a sense of protection and reality, that I was tagged for eternity by the Holy Spirit when I was baptized by the Spirit.

When I was baptized in the Spirit, I was also prayed for. Romans 8:26 says, "Likewise, the Spirit helps us in our weakness. For we do not know what to pray for as we ought." The Holy Spirit prays with groanings that cannot be uttered because he knows our hearts (Rom. 8:26).

And then, at the same time, I was enlightened. I can remember as a boy at a camp going back to my cabin, getting out my Bible, underlining in it, and having the Word come alive to me, as it has continued to come alive in my life. Now when John the Baptist pointedly said, "I baptize you with water, but [Christ] will baptize you with the Holy Spirit and fire," he was talking about the superiority of Jesus's baptism. Water can wash only the outside, but the Spirit and fire regenerate and cleanse the inside. And so that is the great abiding reality and joy of being baptized with the Spirit and fire. The Holy Spirit is making all things new and constantly conforming us to the image of Christ.

Prayer

Lamb of God, our baptism is a sign that we are saved not by our own righteousness, but because we have been given the righteousness of Christ. Let us not make baptism the object of our trust, but look instead to the cleansing work of Jesus, beautifully depicted in baptism. Amen.

Question 46

What is the Lord's Supper?

Christ commanded all Christians to eat bread and to drink from the cup in thankful remembrance of him and his death. The Lord's Supper is a celebration of the presence of God in our midst; bringing us into communion with God and with one another; feeding and nourishing our souls. It also anticipates the day when we will eat and drink with Christ in his Father's kingdom.

📖 1 CORINTHIANS 11:23–26

For I received from the Lord what I also delivered to you, that the Lord Jesus on the night when he was betrayed took bread, and when he had given thanks, he broke it, and said, "This is my body which is for you. Do this in remembrance of me." In the same way also he took the cup, after supper, saying, "This cup is the new covenant in my blood. Do this, as often as you drink it, in remembrance of me." For as often as you eat this bread and drink the cup, you proclaim the Lord's death until he comes.

💬 Commentary

RICHARD BAXTER

O what unspeakable mysteries and treasures of mercy are here presented to us in a sacrament! Here we have communion with a reconciled God, and are brought into his presence by the great Reconciler. Here we have communion with our blessed Redeemer, as crucified and glorified, and offered to us, as our quickening, preserving, strengthening Head. Here we have communion with the Holy Ghost, applying to our souls the benefits of redemption, drawing us to the Son, and communicating light, and life, and strength from him unto us; increasing and actuating his graces in us. Here we have communion with the body of Christ, his sanctified people, the heirs of life. When the minister of Christ by his commission representeth a crucified Christ to our eyes, by the bread and wine appointed to this use, we see Christ crucified as it were before us, and our faith layeth hold on him, and we perceive the truth of the remedy; and build our souls upon this rock. When the same minister by Christ's commission, doth offer us his body, and blood, and benefits, it is as firm and valid to us, as if the mouth of Christ himself had offered them. And when our souls receive him, by that faith which the Holy Ghost exciteth in us, the participation is as true as that of our bodies receiving the bread and wine which represent him.[58]

LIGON DUNCAN

The Lord's Supper is a covenant sign and seal. That means that it both represents and confirms to us the precious promise of God that, through Jesus Christ, he will be our God, and we are his people. In the Lord's Supper we have a remembrance, a celebration of God's presence, and an experience of communion. We also have something that nourishes us, and in the Lord's Supper, we anticipate the glory to come.

First, we have a remembrance in the Lord's Supper. In the Lord's Supper, Jesus told his disciples that they were going to proclaim his death until he comes. The bread and the wine, the body and the blood of Christ in the Lord's Supper, is a representation of a covenant sacrifice. The two constituent parts indicate that Jesus's death was a deliberate act on his part. He gave himself as a sacrifice in our place for the forgiveness of our sins. And so every time we celebrate the Lord's Supper, we are to remember the meaning and significance of the death of Jesus Christ on our behalf. We are to remember him. "Do this in remembrance of me" (Luke 22:19). We celebrate the glorious work of atonement that Jesus Christ accomplished for us.

Second, the Lord's Supper is also a celebration of God's presence. Isn't it amazing that we're invited to slide our knees up under the table of God? That is especially amazing in light of our rebellion. In Genesis 3, Satan said to Eve and to Adam, "Take and eat this fruit." They ate the fruit against God's command, and what was the result? Did it result in their satisfaction and fulfillment? No. It resulted in their being driven away from the presence of God. But at the Lord's Table the Lord himself invites us back into his presence. When Jesus says to his disciples, "Take and eat," he reverses the words of the Serpent in the garden. Derek Kidner has this wonderful line: "God will taste poverty and death before 'take and eat' become verbs of salvation."[59] We experience that every time we come to the Lord's Table, every time we hear the minister say, "Take and eat, all of you." It's a celebration of our reunion with God, his presence with us, and our enjoyment of his near fellowship.

Third, the Lord's Supper is a communion. It's a communion with God and with his people. We not only commune with the living God by grace, we not only commune with the living God by what Jesus has done for us on the cross, but we commune with one another. When we're united to the Lord Jesus Christ, we're united to everyone who is united to the Lord Jesus Christ. That's why Paul says to the Corinthians, "You must discern the body" (1 Cor. 11:29). He's not telling them that they need to understand some mystical thing about the elements in the Lord's Supper. What's the body that he's talking about? The body of Christ, the church, the fellowship of believers.

Finally, the Lord's Supper is spiritual nourishment. It's a means of grace. It's one of God's appointed ways by which he builds us up and nourishes us, confirms our faith, and strengthens us for growth. And the Lord's Supper is an anticipation of the glory to come. Jesus washed his disciples' feet on the night that he was betrayed, and he served them the elements of the Lord's Supper. Interestingly, when Jesus speaks of the marriage supper of the Lamb in consummation (Luke 12:37), in glory, when the great end has come and all have acknowledged him to be King, he says that on that day he will bid us all to recline, just like the disciples reclined on the night of the Lord's Supper, and he will gird himself and serve us.

Yes, in the Lord's Supper, we anticipate the marriage supper of the Lamb, where we will sit down with one another in glory, and our Savior will serve us again everything that we need. What a joy it is to come to the Lord's Table.

Prayer

Bread of Life, we take the Lord's Supper in reverent obedience. We do not want to receive it unworthily, so we come in repentance and faith. Help us to forgive the sins of those who have sinned against us, especially the believers with whom we share the bread and the cup. May our partaking of this meal proclaim your saving death and our desperate need of it. Amen.

Question 47

Does the Lord's Supper add anything to Christ's atoning work?

No, Christ died once for all. The Lord's Supper is a covenant meal celebrating Christ's atoning work; as it is also a means of strengthening our faith as we look to him, and a foretaste of the future feast. But those who take part with unrepentant hearts eat and drink judgment on themselves.

📖 1 PETER 3:18

For Christ also suffered once for sins, the righteous for the unrighteous, that he might bring us to God. . . .

🗩 Commentary

J. C. RYLE

Let us settle it firmly in our minds that the Lord's Supper was not given to be a means either of justification or of conversion. It was never meant to give grace where there is no grace already, or to provide pardon when pardon is not already enjoyed. It cannot possibly provide what is lacking with the absence of repentance to God, and faith toward the Lord Jesus Christ. It is an ordinance for the penitent, not for the impenitent, for the believing, not for the unbelieving, for the converted, not for the unconverted. The unconverted man, who fancies that he can find a shortcut road to heaven by taking the Sacrament, without treading the well-worn steps of repentance and faith, will find to his cost one day that he is totally deceived. The Lord's Supper was meant to increase and help the grace that a man has, but not to impart the grace that he has not. It was certainly never intended to make our peace with God, to justify, or to convert.

The simplest statement of the benefit which a truehearted communicant may expect to receive from the Lord's Supper . . . is the strengthening and refreshing of our souls. Clearer views of Christ and His atonement, clearer views of all the offices which Christ fills as our Mediator and Advocate, clearer views of the complete redemption Christ has obtained for us by His vicarious death on the cross, clearer views of our full and perfect acceptance in Christ before God, fresh reasons for deep repentance for sin, fresh reasons for lively faith, fresh reasons for living a holy, consecrated, Christ-like life,—these are among the leading returns which a believer may confidently expect to get from his attendance at the Lord's Table. He that eats the bread and drinks the wine in a right spirit will find himself drawn into closer communion with Christ, and will feel to know Him more, and understand Him better. . . .

In eating that bread and drinking that cup, such a man will have his repentance deepened, his faith increased, his knowledge enlarged, his habit of holy living strengthened. He will realise more of the "real presence" of Christ in his heart. Eating that bread by faith, he will feel closer communion with the body of Christ. Drinking that wine by faith, he will feel closer communion with the blood of Christ. He will see more clearly what Christ is to him, and what he is to Christ. He will understand more thoroughly what it is to be "one with Christ, and Christ one with him." He will feel the roots of his soul's spiritual life watered, and the work of grace in his heart established, built up, and carried forward. All these things may seem and sound like foolishness to a natural man, but to a true Christian these things are light, and health, and life, and peace.[60]

LEO SCHUSTER

I recently saw a restaurant advertisement that simply had the name of the restaurant and the words *spiritual dining*. It made me wonder about whether dining, at its best, is more than a mere material experience. And it made me think about the Lord's Supper, *the* spiritual meal, and what it does and doesn't do. There are actually three dimensions to what the Lord's Supper does: past, present, and future.

When Jesus instituted the Lord's Supper, he told his disciples, "Do this in remembrance of me" (Luke 22:19), underscoring that what he was urging them to do would point back to what he had done for them. When we remember what Jesus did for us, we ground our lives in his finished work. The Lord's Supper isn't a way you can earn your salvation; it is spiritual dining for those who are saved. It doesn't add anything to the finished work of Christ's once-for-all sacrifice, but confirms and strengthens us in him. It becomes a sort of gospel shorthand where, as an ancient writer put it, first we hear the gospel, then we taste the gospel, and so the gospel goes forward in our lives on two legs. As Paul put it in 1 Corinthians, "For as often as you eat this bread and drink this cup, you proclaim the Lord's death until he comes" (11:26). As Christians we eat and drink to remember Jesus's triumph. That's the past dimension.

Paul points to the present dimension of the Lord's Supper when he writes in 1 Corinthians, "The cup of blessing that we bless, is it not a participation in the blood of Christ? The bread that we break, is it not a participation in the body of Christ?" (10:16). That word *participation* could also be translated "fellowship" or "communion." It's where we get the term *communion*. Think of what that means—the Lord's Supper is not only a symbolic reminder of what Jesus has done for us; it's also a present communion with one another and with Jesus.

It's important to note that the bread and wine don't change in any way. Jesus isn't present physically, but he's present spiritually as the Holy Spirit exhibits him to us by faith. Now for those who are spiritually unresolved, the Lord's Supper is a call to them to receive Christ rather than to participate in the meal. By witnessing Christians partaking, they're encouraged to hear the echo of Jesus's loving call: "I am the bread of life; whoever comes to me shall not hunger, and whoever believes in me shall never thirst" (John 6:35). And when we as believers take communion by faith, Jesus meets with us, uniting us as a community, nourishing us with himself, and strengthening us to love and obey him. That's the present dimension.

When Jesus gave his disciples the cup he said, "I will not drink again of this fruit of the vine until that day when I drink it new with you in my Father's kingdom" (Matt. 26:29). With these words he directed them to the future dimension of the Lord's Supper, as a sign pointing forward to the great day of anticipation. It's a foretaste of the marriage supper of the Lamb and the everlasting feast believers will enjoy with Christ in glory. Now we're broken creatures due to sin. Through Christ's broken body we're made whole again. Yet in this life we continue to experience the brokenness of our fallen condition. The future dimension of the Lord's Supper points us forward in hope to a day when we will be made completely whole and when we'll enjoy, with our Savior and with one another, dining at its very best.

Prayer

Conqueror of Death, we celebrate your finished work when we take the Lord's Supper. May our eating be a confession of faith, that though we are unworthy, we have been joined together with the worthiness of Christ. May we come to your table with repentant hearts, putting away pride and self-sufficiency, enjoying the free grace you offer to us. Amen.

Question 48

What is the church?

God chooses and preserves for himself a community elected for eternal life and united by faith, who love, follow, learn from, and worship God together. God sends out this community to proclaim the gospel and prefigure Christ's kingdom by the quality of their life together and their love for one another.

📖 2 THESSALONIANS 2:13

But we ought always to give thanks to God for you, brothers beloved by the Lord, because God chose you as the firstfruits to be saved, through sanctification by the Spirit and belief in the truth.

💬 Commentary

CHARLES HADDON SPURGEON

My brethren, let me say, be ye like Christ at all times. Imitate him in public. Most of us live in some sort of publicity; many of us are called to work before our fellow-men every day. We are watched; our words are caught; our lives are examined, taken to pieces. The eagle-eyed, argus-eyed world observes everything we do, and sharp critics are upon us. Let us live the life of Christ in public. Let us take care that we exhibit our Master, and not ourselves—so that we can say, "It is no longer I that live, but Christ that lives in me." Take heed that you carry this into the church too. . . . Be like Christ in the church. How many there are of you . . . seeking pre-eminence? How many are trying to have some dignity and power over their fellow Christians, instead of remembering that it is the fundamental rule of all our churches, that there all men are equal—alike brethren, alike to be received as such. Carry out the spirit of Christ, then, in your churches, wherever ye are; let your fellow members say of you, "He has been with Jesus."[61]

JOHN YATES

The church is the family of God. In the New Testament it's called the community of the new covenant. It's the body of which Christ is the Head. It's the bride of Christ. We're called a holy people, a holy nation, a royal priesthood. The church is the people who have been made God's children, adopted by God through Jesus Christ. And the church consists of all cultures, all ethnic groups, people across the ages, all those who have come to know Jesus Christ as Lord.

In my tradition, the Anglican tradition, we have a statement of faith called the Thirty-Nine Articles. They describe the church this way:

> The local, visible church of Christ is a congregation of faithful men and women, in which the pure Word of God is preached and the Sacraments are duly ministered according to Christ's ordinance. . . .
>
> The church has no authority except in submission to Christ, and it is not lawful for the church to ordain anything that is contrary to God's Word written, and neither may it so expound one place of Scripture that it be repugnant to another.[62]

The ancient creeds describe the church as "one holy catholic and apostolic." It is *one* because the church is one body under one head. It is *holy* because the Holy Spirit indwells it and consecrates it, directing the members of the church in the work of God. It is *catholic*, meaning worldwide, proclaiming the whole apostolic faith to all people to the end of time. And it's *apostolic*. That means we continue the teaching and fellowship of the apostles, and we're sent out on Christ's mission to all people.

We don't choose who is going to be in the church, just as we have no say in who our brothers and sisters or cousins are. God chooses. Whatever particular denomination or group they may belong to, God's people are part of the church and our brothers and sisters.

The church is summed up in this wonderful old hymn by Samuel J. Stone:

The church's one foundation
is Jesus Christ her Lord;
she is his new creation
by water and the word.
From heaven he came and sought her
to be his holy bride;
with his own blood he bought her,
and for her life he died.

Elect from every nation,
yet one o'er all the earth;
her charter of salvation,
one Lord, one faith, one birth;
one holy name she blesses,
partakes one holy food,
and to one hope she presses,
with every grace endued.[63]

🙌 Prayer

King Over All, you have brought us together as the family of God. Keep us faithful to worship together, to love one another, and to provide for each other's needs. Let our fellowship be genuine, and help us to spur one another on in the faith. Amen.

Question 49

Where is Christ now?

Christ rose bodily from the grave on the third day after his death and is seated at the right hand of the Father, ruling his kingdom and interceding for us, until he returns to judge and renew the whole world.

📖 EPHESIANS 1:20–21

He raised him from the dead and seated him at his right hand in the heavenly places, far above all rule and authority and power and dominion, and above every name that is named, not only in this age but also in the one to come.

💬 Commentary

CHARLES WESLEY

> Hail the day that sees Him rise,
> Ravish'd from our wishful eyes!
> Christ, awhile to mortals given,
> Re-ascends His native heaven!
>
> There the pompous triumph waits:
> "Lift your heads, eternal gates,

Wide unfold the radiant scene,
Take the King of Glory in!"

Circled round with angel powers,
Their triumphant Lord, and ours,
Conqueror over death and sin,
Take the King of Glory in!

Him though highest heaven receives,
Still He loves the earth He leaves;
Though returning to His throne,
Still He calls mankind His own.

See! He lifts His hands above!
See! He shows the prints of love!
Hark! His gracious lips bestow
Blessings on His church below!

Still for us His death He pleads;
Prevalent, He intercedes;
Near Himself prepares our place,
Harbinger of human race.

Master, (will we ever say,)
Taken from our head to-day;
See Thy faithful servants, see!
Ever gazing up to Thee.

Grant, though parted from our sight,
High above yon azure height,
Grant our hearts may thither rise,
Following Thee beyond the skies.

Ever upward let us move,
Wafted on the wings of love;
Looking when our Lord shall come,
Longing, gasping after home.

There we shall with Thee remain,
Partners of Thy endless reign;
There Thy face unclouded see,
Find our heaven of heavens in Thee![64]

DAVID BISGROVE

No doubt you've heard the phrase "out of sight, out of mind." Someone who's not around, whom you haven't seen in a long time, doesn't have much impact or relevance in your day-to-day life. The Bible tells us that after Jesus's resurrection, he ascended into heaven, disappearing from view, out of sight. But we're also told that because of where he now resides, we can be assured that he's relevant in our daily lives.

So where is Jesus now? He's seated at the right hand of God the Father. But what difference does that make to us in our day-to-day lives? First, it reminds us that Jesus rules over all creation. Psalm 110 paints a beautiful picture of God's enemies as a footstool of Jesus as he sits at the Father's right hand. Can you see the comfort of that in your daily life? When you struggle with discouragement or disappointment or bitterness about the way your life is going, or when you're discouraged and angry about all the injustice and evil in the world, and like David in Psalm 37 you're tempted to ask why the wicked seem to flourish, consider where Jesus is now. He's at the right hand of God the Father. See him there. Enemies are his footstool. The One who conquered death is now ruling the world. Ephesians 1 says that Jesus was given all authority and will one day return and make the crooked places straight. So let where Jesus is now give you hope and courage to trust and follow him.

But there's even more. Not only is Jesus the King who rules, but he is the Priest who intercedes. Hebrews 10 tells us that Jesus is the great High Priest, who on the cross offered himself as the ultimate sacrifice for sin. He is now interceding and praying for us at the Father's right hand. He is our Advocate in every sense of that word. So to see Jesus at God's right hand as our High Priest is to remember that there is no condemnation for our sin, that Jesus sacrificed himself so that we could be united with him. We have the full rights, therefore, as God's children.

So, yes, Jesus is out of sight. We can't physically see him. But he is active in our day-to-day lives and in this world at the right hand of God the Father ruling as our King, interceding as our Priest, and waiting to return, when he will wipe away every tear, beat swords into plowshares, and flood the world with his glory and grace.

Prayer

Risen and Ascended Lord, though you no longer walk this earth, you rule over us from your throne. All authority and power are in you. Your name is above all names. Raise us up at the last day to live with you in your kingdom. Amen.

Question 50

What does Christ's resurrection mean for us?

Christ triumphed over sin and death by being physically resurrected, so that all who trust in him are raised to new life in this world and to everlasting life in the world to come. Just as we will one day be resurrected, so this world will one day be restored. But those who do not trust in Christ will be raised to everlasting death.

📖 1 THESSALONIANS 4:13–14

But we do not want you to be uninformed, brothers, about those who are asleep, that you may not grieve as others do who have no hope. For since we believe that Jesus died and rose again, even so, through Jesus, God will bring with him those who have fallen asleep.

💬 Commentary

MARTYN LLOYD-JONES

The whole creation will have been delivered from the bondage of corruption and will be enjoying "the glorious liberty of the children of God" (Rom. 8:21). Everything will be glorified, even nature itself.

And that seems to me to be the biblical teaching about the eternal state: that what we call heaven is life in this perfect world as God intended humanity to live it. When He put Adam in Paradise at the beginning Adam fell, and all fell with him, but men and women are meant to live in the body, and will live in a glorified body in a glorified world, and God will be with them.[65]

D. A. CARSON

The resurrection of Jesus Christ carries with it many, many wonderful implications. The first is that it vindicates Jesus. In other words, some people thought that if Jesus died on the cross, it could only be because he deserved it. He was declared guilty by a Roman court. And the Old Testament itself insists that anyone who hangs on a tree is under the curse of God. But as it turns out, he did not die as a damned man because of his own sin. Rather, he was bearing the sin of others, and that sacrifice so pleased God that God raised him from the dead. Thus, his resurrection is a form of vindication. It is proof positive that when Jesus said with his dying words, "It is finished," God agreed. His Father agreed. The work of redemption had been accomplished, and the Father vindicates Jesus through the resurrection.

The resurrection also demonstrates the gospel's concern for human beings embodied. In other words, some people think of our ultimate state as kind of ethereal spirit beings without any connection with bodies. But part of elementary, fundamental Christian truth is that in the new heaven and the new earth, the ultimate goal, the home of righteousness, there will not be just heavenly existence. It's earthly existence. It's a new heaven *and a new earth*, and we will have resurrection bodies like Christ's. That's one of the great arguments of 1 Corinthians 15. Paul argues that if Christ rose from the dead in a resurrection body—which, however strange in some ways and remarkable it was, could be touched and handled, could be spoken to, could be seen, and could actually eat human food—then when we, who are finally resurrected on the last day, come into that final state, we will have resurrection bodies like his resurrection body. That is our destination. So his resurrection is the firstfruit of what is often called a general resurrection at the end of the age. All human beings will be resurrected, whether to life or to condemnation, because we are essentially embodied people.

And with this comes also a vision of life and existence beyond this life. We should not think that Christianity merely sorts out some problems in our lives here. Rather, the ultimate goal is beyond this life. When we get older and more hairs fall out and arthritis kicks in, or we slink away into dementia, suddenly resurrection existence begins to look very good indeed because our hope is not to survive to seventy or eighty or even ninety. Our hope finally is a body like Christ's resurrection body. And his is the firstfruit; ours has been secured by him, and we are coming along behind him to join him in resurrection existence: full-bodied resurrection existence in the new heaven and the new earth, the home of righteousness. That's why 1 Thessalonians 4, the great resurrection chapter, ends with the words "Therefore encourage one another with these words."

Prayer

Resurrecting God, make us mindful that death is not the end for us. Save us from the judgment we deserve, and make us faithful to implore others to flee from the wrath to come. We look in hope to the joy that will be ours when, saved from that wrath through the merits of Christ, we will be clothed with resurrected bodies to reign on a renewed earth. Amen.

Question 51

Of what advantage to us is Christ's ascension?

Christ physically ascended on our behalf, just as he came down to earth physically on our account, and he is now advocating for us in the presence of his Father, preparing a place for us, and also sends us his Spirit.

📖 ROMANS 8:34

Who is to condemn? Christ Jesus is the one who died—more than that, who was raised—who is at the right hand of God, who indeed is interceding for us.

💬 Commentary

CHARLES WESLEY

> Arise, my soul, arise! Shake off thy guilty fears;
> The bleeding Sacrifice in my behalf appears.
> Before the throne my Surety stands;
> My name is written on his hands.

He ever lives above, for me to intercede,
His all-redeeming love, his precious blood to plead.
His blood atoned for all our race,
And sprinkles now the throne of grace.

Five bleeding wounds he bears, received on Calvary;
They pour effectual prayers, they strongly plead for me:
"Forgive him, oh, forgive!" they cry,
"Nor let that ransomed sinner die."

My God is reconciled; his pardoning voice I hear.
He owns me for his child; I can no longer fear.
With confidence I now draw nigh,
And "Father, Abba Father!" cry.[66]

BRYAN CHAPELL

The ascension is Christ's enthronement as King over all. When he ascended, he showed that he ruled over death and that he continues to assume his place of authority over all the world. The very One who created the world is the One who continues to rule it by the word of his power.

Now when we say that Christ rules, we mean that in his ascension he assumed the office of King that he had before he came to earth. While on this earth, he continued to maintain all things and accomplish all his purposes, even to his death and resurrection. But as now the ascended Lord, he is Lord over all. He is the One who controls all things so that they are working for the good of those who love him.

But he's not simply King. He, in his ascension, is interceding for us at the right hand of God. He continues to fulfill the office of a priest as well, providing what is needed as advocacy and intercession before the Father. As we repent of our sins, as we pray to God, our sins are taken by the Son of God, acting as a priest on our behalf, as the One who now intercedes for us, so that God will listen and act in our behalf.

Not only is Jesus acting as that King and as Priest in our behalf, he continues to send his Word into our hearts by the work of his

Spirit. The Holy Spirit, remember, was to testify of Christ. The very reason that we can understand God's Word—not just its logic but its significance—is that the Holy Spirit sent by Christ himself is opening our hearts to it. This means that as that Word comes from Christ and is given to us by his Spirit, Jesus continues to operate as a prophet on our behalf, giving us the Word of God so that we can walk with him, understand him, and understand his grace.

All this means that Christ in his ascension is operating for our present good. He's ruling our present circumstances. He's advocating for us in our present circumstances. He's sending his Word into our hearts so that we can handle our present circumstances. But that's not the end of his job.

As Prophet, Priest, and King, he's also preparing for our future. All things are being worked toward a divine end, a culmination, a consummation of the glory of God by the One who rules over all for the purposes that he has designed. He, as King, is preparing a place for us of God's great blessing. As Priest he is going to ensure that when we stand before the throne of judgment, we will be made right before God by the cleansing work of his blood. Jesus's priestly nature will again come to the fore as we bow before the Lamb of God, who by his blood purchased men and women for God from every tribe and language and people and nation. That priestly role Christ will also fulfill as he prepares a future for us. And, ultimately by his Spirit, he will secure all who are his own. So that God by his Spirit is accomplishing his will not only in the present world but also in eternity. He is securing by the power of the Spirit all that God intends, sent by the purposes, power, and ultimate love of Jesus Christ.

That ascended Lord is the One who, by being Prophet, Priest, and King, is ruling over our present and preparing for our future.

Prayer

Interceding Savior, you have not stopped showing compassion for your people. You were tempted in every way as we are, and you now intercede for us when we are tempted. Plead for us to your Father, for you are our advocate before the judge of all the earth. Amen.

Question 52

What hope does everlasting life hold for us?

It reminds us that this present fallen world is not all there is; soon we will live with and enjoy God forever in the new city, in the new heaven and the new earth, where we will be fully and forever freed from all sin and will inhabit renewed, resurrection bodies in a renewed, restored creation.

📖 REVELATION 21:1–4

Then I saw a new heaven and a new earth, for the first heaven and the first earth had passed away, and the sea was no more. And I saw the holy city, new Jerusalem, coming down out of heaven from God, prepared as a bride adorned for her husband. And I heard a loud voice from the throne saying, "Behold, the dwelling place of God is with man. He will dwell with them, and they will be his people, and God himself will be with them as their God. He will wipe away every tear from their eyes, and death shall be no more, neither shall there be mourning, nor crying, nor pain anymore, for the former things have passed away."

⊟ Commentary

J. C. RYLE

Let us settle it then in our minds, for one thing, that the *future happiness* of those who are saved is eternal. However little we may understand it, it is something which will have no end: it will never cease, never grow old, never decay, never die. At God's "right hand are pleasures for evermore" (Ps. 16:11). Once landed in paradise, the saints of God shall go out no more. The inheritance is "incorruptible, undefiled, and fadeth not away." They shall "receive a crown of glory that fadeth not away" (1 Pet. 1:4; 5:4). Their warfare is accomplished; their fight is over; their work is done. They shall hunger no more, neither thirst any more. They are travelling on towards an "eternal weight of glory," towards a home which shall never be broken up, a meeting without a parting, a family gathering without a separation, a day without night. Faith shall be swallowed up in sight, and hope in certainty. They shall see as they have been seen, and know as they have been known, and "be for ever with the Lord." I do not wonder that the apostle Paul adds, "Comfort one another with these words" (1 Thess. 4:17–18).[67]

TIMOTHY KELLER

The catechism answer tells us two things about the glorious future that the gospel assures us is coming.

First, we are going to enjoy God forever. Because God is triune within himself, Father, Son, and Holy Spirit have been glorifying each other, delighting in each other, adoring each other, loving each other. Therefore, God within himself has infinite joy. And we were created to share in that joy. We were created to glorify him and to participate in that glory and joy. But none of us, even the strongest Christians today, have ever experienced what that joy is—perfect, cosmic, infinite, endlessly growing—because all of us worship and adore other things. Someday we will be freed from sin, and then we will know and experience that glory and joy. We will enjoy him forever.

Second, we will enjoy him forever in the new city, in the New Jerusalem, in the new heavens and new earth. We will experience this cosmic joy not in a purely immaterial condition. But, rather, we will be in a restored material creation. We will have resurrection bodies like Jesus's body—physical bodies. And what that means is, as Christianity envisions, the body and the soul, the physical and the spiritual, are together in perfect harmony forever. No other religion envisions that. We will not float about as disembodied spirits, but we will dance. We will march. We will hug. We will be embraced. We will eat, and we will drink in the kingdom of God. It means all of our deepest longings will be fulfilled. All of our greatest sorrows will be swallowed up.

What could be better than that? And that's what we're in for. Nothing less.

Prayer

Eternal God, we eagerly await the fullness of your kingdom. We long for every tear to be dried. We groan for the day when we no longer struggle against the flesh. Let the sure hope of everlasting life give us courage to face the trials of this life. Amen. Come, Lord Jesus!

Historical Commentators

Athanasius of Alexandria (296–373) was an early church bishop who has been called the "Father of Orthodoxy" because he led the fight against the Arian heresy. He took part in the First Council of Nicaea (325) and was exiled from his home and ministry five different times because of political and theological controversies.

Augustine of Hippo (354–430) was bishop of Hippo in Roman North Africa, a philosopher, and a theologian. He wrote an account of his conversion in his *Confessions*, his best-known work. But he was also one of the most prolific Latin authors in terms of surviving works, with hundreds of separate titles (including apologetic works, texts on Christian doctrine, and commentaries) and more than 350 preserved sermons.

Richard Baxter (1615–1691), an English Puritan, served as a chaplain in the army of Oliver Cromwell and as a pastor in Kidderminster. When James II was overthrown, Baxter was persecuted and imprisoned for eighteen months. He continued to preach, later writing, "I preached as never sure to preach again, and as a dying man to dying men." In addition to his theological works, he wrote poems, hymns, and his own Family Catechism.

Abraham Booth (1734–1806), an English Baptist minister, served as pastor of Prescot Street Church in Whitechapel, London, for thirty-five years. He also founded what is now Regents Park College for ministerial training in Oxford. He is most known for his work *The Reign of Grace*.

John Bradford (1510–1555) was an English Protestant Reformer who studied at Cambridge University and was made royal chaplain to King Edward VI. When Catholic Mary Tudor came to the throne, Bradford was arrested along with Bishops Latimer and Ridley and Archbishop Cranmer. Bradford had a great reputation as a preacher, and a vast crowd came to his execution. He is most remembered for his statement "There but for the grace of God goes John Bradford." His works, some of which were written from prison, include letters, exhortations, eulogies, meditations, sermons, and essays.

John Bunyan (1628–1688), known as the tinker of Elstow, underwent a dramatic conversion and became a leading Puritan preacher. As his popularity grew, Bunyan became a target for slander and libel and was eventually imprisoned. While in prison he commenced his best-known work, *The Pilgrim's Progress*, first printed in 1678.

John Calvin (1509–1564), a theologian, administrator, and pastor, was born in France into a strict Roman Catholic family. Calvin worked most of his life in Geneva and organized the Reformed church. He wrote the *Institutes of the Christian Religion*, the Geneva Catechism, and numerous commentaries on Scripture.

Oswald Chambers (1874–1917) was a Scottish minister, best known for the devotional classic *My Utmost for His Highest*. He founded a Bible college in London and served as a YMCA chaplain during World War I. After he died on assignment in Cairo, his widow compiled and published *My Utmost for His Highest* based on her transcriptions of his sermons.

John Chrysostom (347–407) was archbishop of Constantinople. Born in Antioch, he was given the title Chrysostom, which means "golden mouth," because of his eloquent preaching. He is recognized by the Eastern Orthodox Church and the Catholic Church as a saint and doctor of the church. Chrysostom is known for his *Divine Liturgy of St. John Chrysostom* and his vast homiletical works, including sixty-seven homilies on Genesis, ninety on the Gospel of Matthew, and eighty-eight on the Gospel of John.

Thomas Cranmer (1489–1556) was an English Reformer and the archbishop of Canterbury when the Church of England, under Henry VIII, broke away from Roman Catholicism. In his work to reform the liturgy of the church, he wrote *The Book of Common Prayer*, which still serves as the foundation for Anglican worship today.

Jonathan Edwards (1703–1758) was a colonial American preacher, theologian, and philosopher. Edwards became pastor of the church in Northampton, Massachusetts, in 1726. He is widely known for his sermon "Sinners in the Hands of an Angry God," as well as his many books, including *The End for Which God Created the World* and *A Treatise concerning Religious Affections*. Edwards died from a smallpox inoculation shortly after beginning the presidency at the College of New Jersey (later Princeton University).

George Herbert (1593–1633) was a Welsh-born Anglican priest who posthumously became one of the most beloved poets of the seventeenth century. He gave up a prominent career in oratory to become a rural pastor. Throughout his ministry, he wrote devotional poetry, which was published in a collection titled *The Temple* after his death.

Martyn Lloyd-Jones (1899–1981) was a Welsh medical doctor and Protestant minister. Lloyd-Jones is best known for preaching and teaching at Westminster Chapel in London for thirty years. He would take many months, even years, to expound a chapter of the Bible verse by verse. He is best known for the book *Spiritual Depression*, as well as a fourteen-volume set of commentaries on Romans.

Martin Luther (1483–1546) was a German pastor and professor of theology. His family intended for him to become a lawyer, but he took monastic orders. On October 31, 1517, Luther nailed The Ninety-Five Theses to the door of a church in Wittenberg, sparking the Protestant Reformation. His refusal to retract his writings at the demand of Pope Leo X and Emperor Charles V resulted in his excommunication. Luther wrote many works, including his small and large catechisms, and preached hundreds of sermons in churches and universities.

John Owen (1616–1683) was an English Puritan theologian. He went to Oxford University at age twelve, gained an MA at nineteen, and became a pastor at twenty-one. Years later he was appointed vice-chancellor of the University. He preached to Parliament the day after the execution of King Charles I, fulfilling the task without directly mentioning that event. He wrote numerous and voluminous works, including historical treatises on religion and several studies on the Holy Spirit.

J. C. Ryle (1816–1900) was the first Anglican bishop of Liverpool. Ryle's appointment was at the recommendation of Prime Minister Benjamin Disraeli. As well as being a writer and pastor, Ryle was an athlete who rowed and played cricket for Oxford University. He was responsible for building more than forty churches.

Francis Schaeffer (1912–1984) was an American Presbyterian pastor and philosopher and is most famous for his writing and his establishment of L'Abri ("The Shelter") community in Switzerland. He wrote twenty-two books, the best known being the trilogy *The God Who Is There, Escape from Reason*, and *He Is There and He Is Not Silent*, as well as *A Christian Manifesto*.

Richard Sibbes (1577–1635), an English Puritan theologian, was known as "the Heavenly Doctor Sibbes." A preacher at Gray's Inn, London, and master of Catherine Hall, Cambridge, he was the author of several devotional works, most famously *The Bruised Reed and Smoking Flax*.

Charles Simeon (1759–1836) was rector of Trinity Church, Cambridge, for forty-nine years. Simeon was offered the leadership of the church as he was preparing to graduate from the university. At first, the congregants showed their displeasure at his preaching by frequent interruptions and by locking the small doors of their pews so that no one could sit down. Simeon is best known for his twenty-one-volume *Horae Homilecticae*, a collection of expanded sermon outlines from all sixty-six books of the Bible.

Charles Haddon Spurgeon (1834–1892), an English Baptist preacher, became pastor of London's New Park Street Church (later Metropolitan Tabernacle) at twenty years old. He frequently preached to more than ten thousand people with no electronic amplification. Spurgeon was a prolific writer, and his printed works are voluminous. He preached nearly thirty-six hundred sermons and published forty-nine volumes of commentaries, sayings, hymns, and devotions.

Charles Wesley (1707–1788) was a pastor in the Church of England and the writer of many beloved hymns, including "Christ the Lord Is Risen Today," "And Can It Be That I Should Gain?" and "Hark! the Herald Angels Sing." With his brother John, he was an early leader in the Methodist movement.

John Wesley (1703–1791), an English preacher and theologian, is largely credited with founding the English Methodist movement. He traveled on horseback, preaching two or three times each day, and is said to have preached more than forty thousand sermons. He was also a noted hymn writer.

Contemporary Contributors

Thabiti Anyabwile is pastor of Anacostia River Church in Washington, DC. Prior to that, he served as the pastor of First Baptist Church of Grand Cayman for seven years. He is a council member of The Gospel Coalition (TGC). Among his other books, he has written *Reviving the Black Church* and *What Is a Healthy Church Member?*

Alistair Begg is senior pastor of Parkside Church near Cleveland, Ohio, and a TGC council member. He has written several books, most recently *Lasting Love: How to Avoid Marital Failure*. Begg can be heard daily and weekly on the radio program *Truth for Life*.

David Bisgrove is lead pastor for the Westside congregation of Redeemer Presbyterian Church in Manhattan. Before becoming a pastor, he worked in healthcare finance and administration.

D. A. Carson is research professor of New Testament at Trinity Evangelical Divinity School in Deerfield, Illinois. He is also president of The Gospel Coalition. He has written numerous books, including *The Intolerance of Tolerance*, *Exegetical Fallacies*, and *Christ and Culture Revisited*.

Bryan Chapell is senior pastor of Grace Presbyterian Church in Peoria, Illinois. He previously served as president of Covenant Theological Seminary for sixteen years. Chapell has written numerous books including *Christ-Centered Preaching* and *Christ-Centered Worship*. He is a TGC council member.

Mark Dever is senior pastor of Capitol Hill Baptist Church in Washington, DC, and president of 9Marks, as well as a TGC council member. Dever is the author of many books, including *Nine Marks of a Healthy Church*.

Kevin DeYoung is senior pastor of University Reformed Church in East Lansing, Michigan, and a TGC council member. His many books include *The Hole in Our Holiness* and *Taking God at His Word*.

Ligon Duncan is chancellor and CEO of Reformed Theological Seminary, president of the Alliance of Confessing Evangelicals, and a TGC council member. He has written or contributed to many books, including *The Unadjusted Gospel*.

Mika Edmondson is founding pastor of New City Fellowship in Southeast Grand Rapids. He completed a doctorate in systematic theology with a dissertation on Martin Luther King Jr.'s theology of suffering.

Collin Hansen is editorial director for The Gospel Coalition and was previously an associate editor for *Christianity Today*. His most recent book is *Blind Spots: Becoming a Courageous, Compassionate, and Commissioned Church*.

R. Kent Hughes is professor of practical theology at Westminster Theological Seminary in Philadelphia and a TGC council member. For twenty-seven years he served as senior pastor of College Church in Wheaton, Illinois. He has written more than thirty books, including *Disciplines of a Godly Man* and *Liberating Ministry from the Success Syndrome*, and is senior editor of the Preaching the Word commentary series.

Timothy Keller is senior pastor of Redeemer Presbyterian Church in Manhattan and vice president of The Gospel Coalition. He has written numerous books, including *The Reason for God* and *The Meaning of Marriage*.

John Lin is lead pastor for the Downtown congregation of Redeemer Presbyterian Church in Manhattan. Before coming to Redeemer, he served as the English-ministry pastor at a Korean-American church.

Vermon Pierre is lead pastor for preaching and mission at Roosevelt Community Church in Phoenix, Arizona, and a TGC council member. He is the author of *Gospel Shaped Living*, part of the Gospel Shaped Church curriculum.

John Piper is founder and teacher of desiringGod.org and chancellor of Bethlehem College & Seminary in Minneapolis, Minnesota. He served as pastor of Bethlehem Baptist Church for thirty-three years. He is a TGC council member and the author of more than fifty books, including *Desiring God*.

Juan Sanchez is the senior pastor of High Pointe Baptist Church in Austin, Texas, and a TGC council member. He is the author of *1 Peter for You*.

Leo Schuster is lead pastor of City Church Houston. He previously served on the pastoral staff of Redeemer Presbyterian Church in Manhattan.

Sam Storms is lead pastor for preaching and vision at Bridgeway Church in Oklahoma City and president of the Evangelical Theological Society. He is a TGC council member and the author of many books, including *Packer on the Christian Life* and *Pleasures Evermore*.

Stephen Um is senior minister of City Life Presbyterian Church in Boston and associate training director for Redeemer City to City. He is a TGC council member and the author of *Why Cities Matter*, as well as *1 Corinthians* in Crossway's Preaching the Word series.

John Yates is rector of The Falls Church Anglican in Northern Virginia. He is a TGC council member and has been active in the Anglican renewal movement in the United States.

Acknowledgments

Bringing *The New City Catechism* (NCC) to print has been a group project over many years. Tim Keller, Sam Shammas, and Redeemer Presbyterian Church deserve credit for their work to adapt the original fifty-two NCC questions and answers from Calvin's Geneva Catechism, the Westminster Shorter and Larger Catechisms, and especially the Heidelberg Catechism. Ben Peays spearheaded the online launch as executive director of the Gospel Coalition, and his enthusiasm for this project continues to spur us on. Crossway has been a faithful partner in this venture to reinvigorate the practice of catechesis in our churches and homes. Without the excellent work of Betsy Childs Howard we never could have conceived of this book that we hope will serve individuals, families, and churches for generations to come.

We dedicate this book to mothers, both spiritual and biological, that their children might rise up and call them blessed (Prov. 31:28) as they call on the name of the Lord for salvation (Rom. 10:13).

Collin Hansen, General Editor

Notes

1. Gary Parrett and J. I. Packer, *Grounded in the Gospel: Building Believers the Old-Fashioned Way* (Grand Rapids, MI: Baker, 2010), 16.
2. John Calvin, *Institutes of the Christian Religion*, ed. John T. McNeill, trans. Ford Lewis Battles (Philadelphia: Westminster, 1960), 3.7.1.
3. Jonathan Edwards, *The Works of Jonathan Edwards*, ed. Edward Hickman (London: Ball, Arnold, and Co., 1840), 2:511.
4. Richard Baxter, "The Catechising of Families" in *The Practical Works of the Rev. Richard Baxter*, vol. 19 (London: Paternoster, 1830), 33, 62, 89.
5. J. C. Ryle, *Expository Thoughts on the Gospels: St. Matthew* (New York: Robert Carter & Brothers, 1870), 51, 336–37.
6. John Calvin, *Hebrews*, in Calvin's Commentaries, vol. 22 (Grand Rapids, MI: Eerdmans, 1996), 266. Also available at Christian Classics Ethereal Library, http://www.ccel.org/ccel/calvin/calcom44.xvii.ii.html.
7. Richard Sibbes, *Divine Meditations and Holy Contemplations* (London: J. Buckland, 1775), 13, 114.
8. John Wesley, "The Two Great Commandments" in *Renew My Heart* (Uhrichsville, OH: Barbour, 2011).
9. John Bunyan, "The Doctrine of the Law and Grace Unfolded" in *The Works of that Eminent Servant of Christ, Mr. John Bunyan*, vol. 3 (Edinburgh: Sands, Murray & Cochran, 1769), 245–47.
10. C. H. Spurgeon, "Heart-Knowledge of God" in *The Metropolitan Tabernacle Pulpit: Sermons Preached and Revised by C. H. Spurgeon During the Year 1874*, vol. 20 (London: Passmore & Alabaster, 1875), 674–75.
11. Augustine, *Confessions*, trans. Henry Chadwick (Oxford: Oxford University Press, 1991), 3.
12. John Calvin, *Institutes of the Christian Religion*, trans. Henry Beveridge (Grand Rapids, MI: Eerdmans, 1989), 2.8.2.
13. Martyn Lloyd-Jones, *The Cross* (Wheaton, IL: Crossway, 1986), 176–77.
14. Martin Luther, *Treatise Concerning Good Works* (1520; repr., Brooklyn, NY: Sheba Blake Publishing, 2015), sections 10–11.
15. See section 1, "The Ten Commandments" of Martin Luther's Small Catechism, http://bookofconcord.org/smallcatechism.php#tencommandmentsthe/.

16. John Bradford, "Godly Meditations: A Meditation upon the Ten Commandments," in *The Writings of John Bradford*, ed. Aubrey Townsend (Cambridge: University Press, 1868), 170–71, 172.

17. John Owen, "The Nature, Power, Deceit, and Prevalency of the Remainders of Indwelling Sin in Believers," in *The Works of John Owen*, ed. Thomas Russell, vol. 13 (London: Richard Baynes, 1826), 200–201.

18. Ibid., 26.

19. Abraham Booth, "Confession of Faith," in *Works of Abraham Booth: Late Pastor of the Baptist Church*, vol. 1 (London: Button, 1813), xxxi–xxxii.

20. *Memoirs of the Life of the Rev. Charles Simeon* (London: Hatchard and Son, 1847), 661–62.

21. Oswald Chambers, entry for October 7, *My Utmost for His Highest: Selections for Every Day* (Uhrichsville, Ohio: Barbour, 1992), 207.

22. Martin Luther, *Luther's Large Catechism*, trans. F. Samuel Janzow (St. Louis, MO: Concordia, 1978), 13–17.

23. C. H. Spurgeon, "Hope for the Worst Backsliders," sermon 2452 in *The Complete Works of C. H. Spurgeon*, vol. 42 (Morrisville, PA: Delmarva Publications, 2013). Also available at Bible Bulletin Board, http://www.biblebb.com/files/spurgeon/2452.htm.

24. Jonathan Edwards, *A Treatise Concerning Religious Affections* (Philadelphia: James Crissy, 1821), 48–49.

25. John Chrysostom, "Christmas Morning," in *The Sunday Sermons of the Great Fathers*, vol. 1 (Swedesboro, NJ: Preservation Press, 1996), 110–115.

26. St. Augustine, *Sermons on the Liturgical Seasons*, sermon 191, in *The Fathers of the Church*, trans. Sister Mary Sarah Muldowney (Washington, D.C., Catholic University of America Press, 1959), 28–29.

27. Athanasius, "On the Incarnation of the Word," in *Athanasius: Select Works and Letters*, vol. 4 of *The Nicene and Post-Nicene Fathers*, Series 2, ed. Philip Schaff and Henry Wace (Peabody, MA: Hendrickson, 1999), 40–41.

28. John Chrysostom, "Easter Sermon by John Chrysostom," in *Service Book of the Holy Orthodox-Catholic Apostolic (Greco-Russian) Church*, trans. Isabel Florence Hapgood (New York: Riverside Press, 1906), 235–36.

29. Athanasius, "On the Incarnation of the Word," in *Athanasius: Select Works and Letters*, vol. 4 of *The Nicene and Post-Nicene Fathers*, Series 2, ed. Philip Schaff and Henry Wace (Peabody, MA: Hendrickson, 1999), 40.

30. Richard Sibbes, "Of Confirming this Trust in God," in *The Soul's Conflict and Victory over Itself by Faith* (London: Pickering, 1837), 325–26.

31. Augustus Toplady, "Rock of Ages," 1763.

32. John Bunyan, *Heart's-Ease in Heart-Trouble* (London: John Baxter, 1804), 60.

33. Martyn Lloyd-Jones, "Creation and Common Grace," in *God the Holy Spirit*, vol. 2 of *Great Doctrines of the Bible* (Wheaton, IL: Crossway, 2003), 24–25.

34. Richard Mouw, *He Shines in All That's Fair* (Grand Rapids, MI: Eerdmans, 2001), 14.

35. J. C. Ryle, *Consider Your Ways* (London: Hunt & Son, 1849), 23–24.

36. C. H. Spurgeon, entry for September 25 morning, in *Morning by Morning* (New York: Sheldon and Company, 1866), 269.

37. Jonathan Edwards, *The Works of Jonathan Edwards*, ed. Edward Hickman (London: Ball, Arnold, and Co., 1840), 2:580.

38. John Wesley, "Letter to the Rev. Dr. Middleton," in *The Works of the Reverend John Wesley*, vol. 5 (New York: Emory & Waugh, 1831), 757.

39. Abraham Booth, *The Reign of Grace: From Its Rise to Its Consummation* (Glasgow: Collins, 1827), 247–48.

40. John Calvin, "The Necessity of Reforming the Church," in *Theological Treatises*, ed. and trans. J. K. S. Reid, *The Library of Christian Classics* (Louisville: WJKP, 1954), 199.

41. Edward Mote, "My Hope Is Built on Nothing Less," 1834.

42. C. H. Spurgeon, "The Agreement of Salvation by Grace with Walking in Good Works," sermon 2210 in *The Complete Works of C. H. Spurgeon*, vol. 37 (Morrisville, PA: Delmarva Publications, 2015). Also available at Bible Bulletin Board, http://www.biblebb.com/files/spurgeon/2210.htm.

43. Francis A. Schaeffer, *The God Who Is There*, in *The Francis A. Schaeffer Trilogy: The Three Essential Books in One Volume* (Wheaton, IL: Crossway, 1990), 182–83.

44. St. Augustine, *The City of God*, trans. Marcus Dods (Digireads, 2009), 329–30.

45. Gordon D. Fee, "On Getting the Spirit Back into Spirituality," in *Life in the Spirit*, ed. Jeffrey Greenman and George Kalantzis (Downers Grove, IL: InterVarsity Press, 2010), 43.

46. Thomas F. Torrance, *The Trinitarian Faith* (London: T & T Clark, 1991), 191.

47. John Owen, "The Indwelling of the Spirit," in *The Doctrine of the Saints' Perseverance Explained and Confirmed*, vol. 11 of *The Works of John Owen*, ed. William Goold (New York: Robert Carter & Brothers, 1853), 343–61.

48. Abraham Booth, "The Reign of Grace," in *Booth's Select Works* (London: Chidley, 1839), 187–88.

49. "Mr. John Bunyan's Dying Saying: Of Prayer," in *The Works of That Eminent Servant of Christ John Bunyan*, vol. 1 (Philadelphia: John Ball, 1850), 47.

50. John Chrysostom, "Homily 37: On John," in *Commentary on Saint John the Apostle and Evangelist, Homilies 1–47*, vol. 33 of *The Fathers of the Church*, trans. Sister Thomas Aquinas Goggin (Washington, DC, Catholic University Press, 1957), 359.

51. Martin Luther, *Commentary on the Sermon on the Mount*, trans. Charles A. Hay (Philadelphia: Lutheran Publication Society, 1892), 246.
52. Thomas Cranmer, "Thomas Cranmer's Preface to the Great Bible," in *Miscellaneous Writings and Letters of Thomas Cranmer*, ed. J. E. Cox (Cambridge: Cambridge University Press, 1846), 122.
53. Charles Simeon, "The Bible Standard of Religion," in *Horae Homilecticae: or Discourses (Principally in the Form of Skeletons) and Forming a Commentary upon Every Book of the Old and New Testament*, vol. 3 (London: Holdsworth & Ball, 1832), 542–43.
54. Westminster Confession of Faith, 27.1.
55. J. I. Packer, *Concise Theology* (Wheaton, IL: Tyndale, 1993), 210.
56. "Holy Baptism (I)" in *The Poems of George Herbert* (London: Walter Scott, 1885), 35–36.
57. John Calvin, *Calvin's Bible Commentaries: Matthew, Mark and Luke*, part 1, trans. John King (London: Forgotten Books, 2007), 187.
58. Richard Baxter, "A Saint or a Brute," in *The Practical Works of Richard Baxter*, vol. 10 (London: Paternoster, 1830), 318–19.
59. Derek Kidner, *Genesis*, Tyndale Old Testament Commentaries (Downers Grove, IL: IVP Academic), 73.
60. J. C. Ryle, "Thoughts on the Supper of the Lord," in *Principles for Churchmen* (London: William Hunt, 1884), 267–70.
61. Charles Haddon Spurgeon, "Christ's People—Imitators of Him," in *Sermons of the Rev. C. H. Spurgeon* (New York: Sheldon, Blakeman & Co., 1858), 263–64.
62. Articles 19 and 20 of the Thirty-Nine Articles.
63. Samuel J. Stone, "The Church's One Foundation," 1866.
64. Charles Wesley, "Hail the Day That Sees Him Rise," 1739.
65. Martyn Lloyd-Jones, "The Final Destiny," in *The Church and the Last Things*, vol. 3 of *Great Doctrines of the Bible* (Wheaton, IL: Crossway, 2003), 247–48.
66. Charles Wesley, "Arise, My Soul, Arise," 1742.
67. J. C. Ryle, *Practical Religion* (Grand Rapids, MI: Baker, 1977), 476. Available at Project Gutenberg, http://www.gutenberg.org/files/38162/38162-h/38162-h.htm#XXI.

THE GOSPEL **COALITION**

The Gospel Coalition is a fellowship of evangelical churches deeply committed to renewing our faith in the gospel of Christ and to reforming our ministry practices to conform fully to the Scriptures. We have committed ourselves to invigorating churches with new hope and compelling joy based on the promises received by grace alone through faith alone in Christ alone.

We desire to champion the gospel with clarity, compassion, courage, and joy—gladly linking hearts with fellow believers across denominational, ethnic, and class lines. We yearn to work with all who, in addition to embracing our confession and theological vision for ministry, seek the lordship of Christ over the whole of life with unabashed hope in the power of the Holy Spirit to transform individuals, communities, and cultures.

Join the cause and visit TGC.org for fresh resources that will equip you to love God with all your heart, soul, mind, and strength, and to love your neighbor as yourself.

TGC.org

Build a framework for understanding core Christian beliefs.

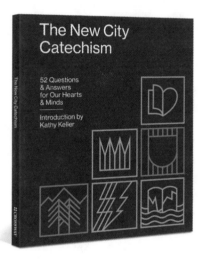

Throughout the history of the church, Christians have used catechisms – collections of questions and answers designed for memorization and recitation – to teach others the core doctrines of the faith. The New City Catechism is a modern-day resource aimed at reintroducing this ancient method of teaching to Christians today.

This short book lays out fifty-two questions and answers related to God, human nature, sin, Christ, the Holy Spirit, and more. Whether used devotionally, recited orally, or memorized over the course of a year, families, churches, small groups, and Christian schools will treasure this as a valuable tool for teaching the core doctrines of the Christian faith to children and adults alike.

For additional resources, see
www.newcitycatechism.com